HO

START A

SENTENCE

WORDS TO BEGIN

SENTENCES

MANIK JOSHI

<u>Dedication</u>

THIS BOOK IS

DEDICATED

TO THOSE

WHO REALIZE

THE POWER OF ENGLISH

AND WANT TO

LEARN IT

SINCERELY

Copyright Notice

****

IMPORTANT NOTE

This Book is Part of a Series
SERIES Name: "English Daily Use"
[A Thirty-Book Series]
BOOK Number: 01
BOOK Title: "How to Start a Sentence"

****

Table of Contents

How to Start a Sentence

There are different ways to start a sentence in English. Using pronoun (I, we, you, they, he, she, it) is the most popular way to begin a sentence. But there are many other words which are widely used to start a sentence. They might be question words (what, where, etc.). They might be words formed from verbs, ending in –ing, -ed, -en, etc. Besides, words such as 'to' 'in' 'with', 'if', 'after' are also used to begin a sentence.

Here, you will learn various words and phrases to start a sentence with.

Important Note:
Starting a sentence with 'and' or 'but' is correct or not!

Using '**And**' or '**But**' to begin a sentence is generally considered grammatically Incorrect. But there is no hard and fast rule in this regard. So, you can use *'And'* or *'But'* to begin a sentence. But avoid excessive use of these words to begin a sentence. Use these words in the beginning of a sentence only when they really give strength to your language.

Note: It is said that a sentence should not be begun with a conjunction of any kind, especially one of the FANBOYS (for, and, nor, but, or, yet, so). But this is not hard and fast rule. Particularly in spoken English, starting a sentence with 'And' or 'But' is common.

How to Start a Sentence -- Using 'AS'

As a kid I recall jumping over walls.

As a matter of fact no notice was given to anyone.

As a person ages, his body weakens physically.

As a policeman myself, I am aware of all the laws.

As against last time four days, the fair will last for five days this year.

As always, he won the match.

As an interim arrangement, he directed the authorities not to return the land.

As fate would have it, he crossed the international border.

As for David, he is doing fine.

As for the difficulty in searching for the honest people, it is not such a big task.

As he got busy, she picked up his son.

As he grew older, he developed his communications skills.

As if the bad power situation in the city wasn't enough, the hike in power tariff has come as the last straw for residents.

As in the past, party president distanced herself from the government's unpopular decision.

As long as here is violence by unruly mobs, use of police force is inevitable.

As news of PM's hospitalization spread, fans and admirers began lining up outside the hospital.

As of now, they have not found any evidence against him.

As often happened, he forgot to send me reply.

As part of the deal, they will hand-over control of five towns.

As penance, he vowed to never scold any kid ever again.

As per his version, nobody had got injured in the incident.

As per rules, the same bill should be passed by the two Houses of the Parliament before it is sent to the President for his signature and promulgation for implementation.

As sanitary workers are absent on most of the days, sweeping of roads are also irregular resulting in trash along the road.

As the bus was nearing, / **As the bus neared** him, he moved aside.

As the day progressed, over a hundred men protestors gathered at the office.

As the electric cables are hanging loosely, it may anytime lead to major accident if any passer-by comes into contact.

As the forces were conducting search, the militants fired upon them, triggering an encounter.

As the mercury levels are dropping each day, difficulties for the poor are constantly rising.

As the news of a leopard in the area spread, onlookers gathered at the site.

As the situation in the town worsened, jittery people rushed back to their homes.

As the war widened, they had to leave the city.

As the winter season approaches, people bring out their blankets to be used in the upcoming days.

As we grow older, we are more in control of our lives.

As we progresses, it is going to become more and more difficult.

As you know, I have sent him a letter.

ADDITIONAL EXAMPLES:

As a first step . . .

As a result . . .

As a rule . . .

As an emergency measure . . .

As an example . . .

As an illustration . . .

As another year draws to a close . . .

As being a latest technology . . .

As explained by . . .

As far as this issue goes . . .

As has been reported earlier . . .

As he grew older he waited patiently for a . . .

As identified by . . .

As is the custom . . .

As passions run high over the attack . . .

As per initial evaluation . . .

As per our customs . . .

As per sources . . .

As per the directions . . .

As per the existing condition for grant of monetary allowance to . . .

As per the plan being finalized by us . . .

As per the provision . . .

As the day broke . . .

As the earth/window shook . . .

As the night temperature has dipped sharply following recent rains . . .

As things stand now/today . . .

As things stand, we are not in a positing in which . . .

As time goes by . . .

How to Start a Sentence -- Using 'AFTER' and 'BEFORE'

After a rail derailment, as many as 15 long distance trains were cancelled, ten short-terminated and five diverted.

After being elected, the President becomes apolitical, rising above the level of politics.

After being on the run for several days, he was arrested in his native village.

After being under treatment in a hospital, she has been brought home today.

After he was arrested, police caught another person.

After hours of hard walk on tough mountainous paths, he collapsed due to fatigue.

After I had shut the door, I opened the safe.

After making the guard unconscious, they tried to rob the bank.

After messing up, they wanted me to pay!

After questioning for more than 15 hours, the police are nowhere near unraveling what happened on that fateful night.

After receiving ragging complaint, the college authorities constituted a five-member committee to probe the matter and also gave a police complaint.

After several incidents of theft were reported, officials launched an investigation.

After she left the room, the quarrel broke out again between them.

After spending one whole day without food or water, we had almost lost all hope of returning home safely.

After the cabinet clears the proposal, they can initiate the process for turning it into a reality.

After the information was passed over to airport, anti-hijack and anti-sabotage measures were initiated.

After the slip, he showed good humour and immediately joked about it.

After the thunderstorm, unripe mangoes were strewn all across our fields.

After they came, the lights went out.

After two weeks, rebels tried to expand hold on city.

After undergoing dialysis, a patient usually feels weak and is advised rest.

After winning the toss, India elected Australia to bat first.

Before he came to the U.S., he had done little travelling.

Before moving the court, he had approached the CM.

Before school is out, I will have returned all of my library books.

Before the timer could go off, bomb was defused.

Before we can tell them about the discount, they will have bought the tickets.

ADDITIONAL EXAMPLES:

After a delay of well over three months . . .

After a wait of nearly two decades . . .

After being confined to tier homes for days . . .

After being married . . .

After five months into the present financial year . . .

After five years of negotiations . . .

After going through all the details . . .

After having gone to London . . .

After having worked for a single aim . . .

After initial opposition . . .

After laying the foundation . . .

After over four years of rule . . .

After the court fixed the date . . .

After three months of probe . . .

After work has been done . . .

Before criticizing someone. . .

Before fleeing on motorbikes . . .

Before she sent him message. . .

Before taking decision. . .

Before that . . .

Before the function . . .

Before the polls . . .

Before these suggestions could be implemented . . .

How to Start a Sentence -- Using 'BY'

By all means, people can question your findings.

By and large the elections passed of 'smoothly' barring 'sporadic' incidents of violence.

By axing trees and blasting mountains to build dams and road, the mountains are being weakened.

By dusk, roads started wearing a deserted look.

By grace of God and all your prayers, I am recovered well.

By his own account, he is a scientist.

By its own admission, the CAG came up with some 3000 objections last year.

By law, you can't cast your vote in India until you are 18.

By most account the system passed its first test.

By noon, a drizzle began which soon tuned into a torrent.

By now the work should have been completed but it is nowhere near compulsion.

By sentencing a celebrity, the court has given the message that nobody is above low.

By the end, he was simply broken.

By the time a new chairman gets used to working in many the department, he/she is transferred.

By the time the terrorists were neutralized, eight people had died.

By this time next month, she will be in Canada.

ADDITIONAL EXAMPLES:

By looking at the recent outbreaks in Asia . . .

By no stretch of imagination . . .

By taking the matter to the Senate . . .

By the looks of it . . .

By the time symptoms are evident . . .

By their definition, this includes . . .

By withdrawing their support . . .

<u>How</u> <u>to</u> <u>Start</u> <u>a</u> <u>Sentence</u> -- <u>Using</u> 'FOR/FROM

For $499, which iPhone would you buy?

For 10 years, she kept wandering on roads and surviving on alms.

For a long time I had problems in coping with the failure.

For a massive leap, one always has to go two steps backward.

For a second day, private TV stations were ordered off the air.

For ages, books have always been a source of inspiration for many.

For centuries, diamonds and gold have been considered to be epitome of grandeur.

For lessons in life, you should watch news.

For not claiming the money, he said some formalities were still left.

For quite some time now, he was behaving angrily.

For sure, people have the right to protest any decision in a democracy.

For the bright future of the country, it is the need of the hour to fight against communalism.

For the fourth time running, they have placed their bet on their party president for the upcoming elections.

For the last ten years I have been writing to the railway authorities.

For the past few years, our business has gone downhill.

For the past many years, he has maintained silence over his financial issues.

For the record, he had issued a similar warning earlier.

For the sake of argument, what would you do if I didn't return your documents?

For the sake of dowry, she was burnt.

For the upcoming tourist season, airlines have introduced the same special offers that they did last year.

For the whole of Monday, our city reeled under severe cold conditions.

For us, every day is full of challenges.

From hot words, they came to blows.

From Italy I crossed over into France.

From national icon to a tainted politician, he had seen it all.

From now on, she had her way.

From now on, trucks and dumpers will be permitted to enter city limits after 11 pm and before 6 am, instead of earlier timings of 10 pm to 7am.

From school going children to working professionals, heavy rainfall has become a serious problem for almost one and all.

From the looks of it, it is soft.

From the moment of birth, every human being wants happiness and does not want suffering.

From the next academic session, the education department may make it mandatory for schools to have book banks.

From the point of view of internal security, police need to remain alert to new challenges like cybercrime.

From the US perspective, deal was good.

From then on I know nothing.

From trekking programmes to cultural and bird-watching tours around the city, visitors have varied options to choose from.

ADDITIONAL EXAMPLES:

For example . . .
For instance . . .
For now . . .
For that reason . . .
For the time being . . .
For this purpose . . .
For this reason . . .

<u>How</u> <u>to</u> <u>Start</u> <u>a</u> <u>Sentence</u> -- <u>Using</u> <u>'IF'</u>

If a passenger fails to book a pet for a train journey, then he/she may have to pay many times the amount of actual fare.

If anyone comes, I will show them my new project.

If anything is consumed too much, it could have various impacts on both mental and physical health.

If at all I have to do anything against the system, I will do it openly.

If banks refuse to exchange soiled notes, should they be fined?

If CCTV cameras were installed in these ATMs and guards were deployed, incidents of robberies could have been avoided.

If facing adversity, you can't force yourself to be happy.

If he belonged to the region of the ruling party, he would not have been given such a harsh sentence.

If he can become president, why can't I.

If he had education, he could have argued with police and told them that his arrest was illegal.

If he were here, I would have found him by now.

If his artificial teeth had gone into the windpipe, it would have been fatal for you.

If his children didn't beg, they would be deprived of meal!

If his request for a diplomatic passport and visa accepted, the cost of travelling and other expenditures would have come under the head of the state government.

If his vehicle had met with an accident, he would have informed us.

If I can do it, so can anyone else.

If I were the president, I would have thrown this proposal in the 'dustbin'.

If I were you, I would certainly attend the meeting.

If it is a sin to fight for social justice and rights, then I am a sinner.

If life gives you lemons, open a lemonade stand and start selling lemonade.

If my daughter had got treatment, she would have survived.

If my salary were timely cleared, I would have repaid my loan.

If necessary, she will finish this project within 24 hours.

If official vehicles continue to use pressure horns, will it be relevant to take action against the common man using such horns?

If past history of the ill-fated proposals is taken into account, there is no hope.

If people were to have access to justice, development of basic infrastructure for the judiciary is indispensable.

If planned properly, your plan can help boost growth.

If pollution board has its way, it will cut down on the sound of crackers.

If Prime Minister were bothered about the vote bank, he would not have been able to take tough decisions.

If soldiers wouldn't be there guarding the borders, we wouldn't be here sleeping peacefully.

If the district administration does not take appropriate steps for the conservation of water bodies, the species of aquatic plants will disappear from the district.

If the media had not highlighted our case, we would have perished years ago.

If there is anything you need, just let me know.

If there is corruption, it cannot be covered up.

If they don't make the payments, there are penalties.

If things continue in this manner, by 2030, cycles will be faster mode of transport.

If we don't apply ourselves well, we are bound to lose.

If we follow the same work routine, it becomes monotonous.

If we need be, we will also go in for checking of stocks.

If we only had to deal with ourselves, life would be far too easy.

If you are a part of a great event, it is obvious to think about it again and again.

If you are found using mobile phone while driving, your license may be cancelled.

If you are not satisfied with the facilities, then you can contact me directly.

If you ask me, you should sleep for six hours a day.

If you can bond with the person you disagree with, then you are mature.

If you can do it, we can too.

If you didn't want to speak to the media, you shouldn't have planned an interaction in the first place.

If you go market, buy some vegetables.

If you had a power, what would you change in the way scientific research is being conducted?

If you have more, leave it. **If you need** it, take it.

If you have suggestions, please do offer.

If you invest wisely, you get the chance to make more money.

If you love someone, don't be afraid to show it.

If you need anything at all, any money, anything, just feel free to ask me.

If you offered animal sacrifice, would all your problems vanish?

If you really love your country that much, why don't you prove it?

If you spend more time with your grandparents, you can benefit greatly.

If you want to change your surroundings, you have to first change your own lifestyle.

If you want to get really, really rich, shift your focus from saving to earning,

If you were reborn, would you still choose the life of an author?

If your friend cries and pleads for help, will you refuse to help?

If you've been thinking of buying a computer, now's the right time.

How to Start a Sentence -- Using 'OF/ON/OUT'

Of the 10, 6 are absent.

Of those, 12 reached there.

On attributes 'most valued' in a partner, he put 'taking care of the home', top of the list.

On basis of the findings and suggestions of the enquiry committees, major changes may be introduced in the answer sheets evaluation process.

On being questioned, he cracked up and admitted to being involved in the crime.

On her talks with the captain of national team, she said she is delighted to meet him.

On his part, he said he is doing the best he can.

On hitting the ground, the plane burst into flames.

On inspection of the school, it has found that there was nothing abnormal.

On investigation, it was revealed that they were innocent.

On many occasions I am called a role model.

On seeing her, Christopher wanted to talk her.

On spotting the lion in the park, residents had made frantic calls to the police from 6 am onwards.

On the condition of that he was not photographed, Clark met the reporter.

On the list of possible midair emergencies, airline passengers are instructed on every flight what to do if the cabin pressure suddenly drops.

On the occasion of the annual wildlife week, a naming ceremony was organized for baby elephants by zoo authorities.

On the one hand, technology is infamous for tearing relationships apart, on the other, it also brings people together.

On the one side of the highway is mountain, while on the other side a gorge.

On this occasion, I convey my warm greetings to you.

On whether the risks in aviation market could possibly outweigh its growth potential, she replied in negative.

Out of more than 400 ATMs in the district, only a handful of them were operational, resulting in heavy crowd outside ATMS.

Out of security consideration, we have to put off our journey.

Out of the shock & shame, his family had left the hometown.

Out of trust, he gave her 5 million dollars.

Out-of-court litigation is expected to help reduce the burden on courts.

ADDITIONAL EXAMPLES:

Of the 300 women who died annually for every 100000 live births . . .

On a day of fast moving developments . . .

On asking why she were crying . . .

On being asked when they found time to study . . .

On being informed that . . .

On buying the house . . .

On coming under question of exposing personal user data to . . .

On the contrary . . .

On the drive back from the airport . . .

On the geological impact, Hubert said . . .

On the one hand . . .

On the opening day of a four-day brainstorming camp, he said . . .

On the other hand . . .

On the pretext of introducing him to other personnel . . .

On the top of it . . .

On this count too . . .

On whether he would be suspended or not . . .

On which options score more, Ivan said . . .

Out of respect for the victims . . .

How to Start a Sentence -- Using 'TO'

To assume that just because of someone's age and gender that they don't pose a threat would be misguided and wrong.

To avoid a difficult situation in case of any emergency, remain prepare in advance.

To be honest, I am in a happy place today and have no complaints.

To bring transparency in the working of police force and pave way for healthy police-public relation police department is going to procure body-worn cameras for on-duty policemen to record their actions.

To build an auditorium is expensive.

To call it a rousing reception would be an understatement.

To celebrate the Independence Day, a grand event was organized in the college.

To change the system we will have to give some sacrifices.

To control the outbreak of dengue, fogging is being carried out by the health department.

To counter fog, which severely impacts railway operations, the railway department distributed anti-fog system for the trains.

To deal with the severe water crisis, authorities have decided to implement a rotation policy under which water would be supplied to different localities at different times.

To discourage people from littering in public places, the municipal corporation has started slapping fines on those found throwing garbage in the open.

To do so, all they would need to do is to produce their identity cards.

To do well in their lives, children need all the support that enables them to actualize their potential.

To ease passenger burden on the existing bus stands, State Road Transport Corporation is planning a new bus stand in the city.

To ensure that passengers get adequate health services, authorities should deploy retired Army doctors in community health centers.

To get irritated is normal; to vent your irritability is not.

To her dismay, they did not bother to reply.

To his surprise, there were 100 birds there.

To insulate the common man from the impact of rising oil price, govt. reduced the tax.

To keep your feet soft and clean, be sure to soak them regularly for ten minutes.

To make villains out of all men would be painting the picture in one colour.

To me, the essence of education is — Personality Development.

To meet your targets you need to be loyal own self and not be affected by negativity around you.

To my great surprise and delight, I found my name in the merit list.

To my relief, my boss only scolded me and went away.

To provide relief to farmers affected by natural calamities, the government has decided to give 2% interest subsidy.

To reduce weight, all you need is a well-structured died with a few low-calorie foods.

To rein in communal violence, a state of emergency has been imposed by the government.

To rein in complaints of water contamination, govt. changed the policies.

To run a coalition government, you require a lot of adjustments.

To save the poor from terrible cold, an NGO distributed woolen clothes.

To say I am not worried will not be correct.

To see everyone else prejudiced in so deadly a manner rendered me despairing.

To start with, the permit regime is being dismantled for a year.

To strengthen its disaster response capabilities, the state disaster management department should use drones for mapping and surveying disaster-hit areas.

To the best of my knowledge, it is true.

To the best of my memory, he has never told a lie.

ADDITIONAL EXAMPLES:

To a (pointed) query if his comments were justified, Lara said . . .

To a question that . . .

To add ideas . . .

To be sure . . .

To begin with . . .

To compare and contrast . . .

To conclude . . .

To cut a long story short . . .

To elaborate . . .

To illustrate . . .

To our astonishment . . .

To overcome the deep-seated societal division on the basis of caste and religion . . .

To put it differently . . .

To review . . .

To such a degree . . .

To sum up . . .

To summarize . . .

To that effect (in this regard) . . .

To the delight of our well-wishers

To top it all . . .

To weed out unauthorized cabs from city . . .

How to Start a Sentence -- Using 'IN'

In a bid to check the mayhem created by freely roaming stray cattle on the roads, the municipal corporation has decided to seek approval for five animal shelters in the town.

In a bid to check traffic congestion during the New Year celebrations, the administration started stopping all vehicles outside the town and provided shuttle services to let visitors enter the town.

In a bid to collect comprehensive ground information on a real-time basis, the Tiger Reserve administration initiated an intranet project which has facilities for live-streaming of footage from cameras placed in sensitive points around the reserve.

In a bid to complete the pending syllabus, schools are conducting extra classes.

In a bid to ensure that big cats in Tiger Reserve do not suffer from possible water scarcity, the authorities concerned are installing solar water pumps inside the park to rejuvenate the waterholes.

In a big relief to patients, the paramedical staff, including pharmacists, nurses and lab technicians, who had gone on an indefinite strike, called off their stir yesterday afternoon.

In a bizarre case of man's vengeance against a beast, villagers killed and ate a leopard.

In a blow to automobile firms, apex court banned sale and registration of vehicles, which are not BS-IV compliant.

In a broad overview of the progress in the road and railways sectors, the president called for a consolidated approach to existing projects and working towards their completion within strict timeline.

In a daring heist in broad daylight on the national highway, ten armed man hijacked a taxi, abducted the occupants and made off with 1 million dollars.

In a decision taken by the Cabinet, government decided to withdraw security cover to ex-ministers.

In a few days' time,

In a first such move in the state, the forest department has deployed two drones to locate a man-eater leopard which had attacked a man yesterday.

In a high-voltage drama, a man going through a troubled marriage shot himself.

In a horrific case of a property dispute,

In a hurriedly called press conference, police officer tried to clear all the confusion related to the high-profile case.

In a major relief to commuters, the city bus association has called off their indefinite strike after reaching a consensus with their transport department.

In a major relief to highway widening projects, the Cabinet allowed exemption of environmental clearance requirement for stretches up to 100 miles in length.

In a miraculous save, the conductor and a passenger managed to jump off the bus seconds before it skidded off the mountain road.

In a move that confirmed the strength of the US-UK alliance, Britain had lifted nuclear sanctions on India.

In a move that has sent out a strong message to the employees absent or missing from their duties, the college administration has terminated duties of ten employees.

In a move that will impact salary payments to millions of workers across the country, the government planned to mandate payments directly into their bank accounts against the current practice of paying in cash.

In a move to curb illegal manufacturing and sale of the hormone oxytocin.

In a move to enhance awareness and safety of drugs, the health ministry tightened labeling norms for high-risk medicines.

In a related development, he was sent to oversee rescue operations.

In a relief to him, an officer has written to the higher authorities that complaints against him are inadmissible.

In a relief to homebuyers, authorities have issued a slew of instructions to ensure they receive their flats in an expedition manner.

In a security lapse, a woman broke through police barricades.

In a series of directions to address the lack of medical services in remote areas, a court ordered the government to fill up the vacant posts of specialist doctors in two months.

In a series of steps directed to improve the traffic situation in the city, court ordered the transport department to ensure to shift the toll barriers located inside the town to a location almost 2 km outside.

In a significant bureaucratic reshuffle that was aimed at improving governance, state government transferred many top officers.

In a special drive to crackdown on crime, police have arrested as many as 500 persons involved in various criminal activities across the state.

In a startling claim, he went public with his allegation that he has been offered bribe of one million dollars.

In a step aimed at curbing the movement of 15-year-old petrol vehicles, the Road Transport Corporation managing director asked the regional managers to take the buses off the road with immediate effect.

In a stringent anti-poaching measure, authorities at tiger reserve had issued shoot-at-sight orders.

In a strongly worded statement, an army officer said the terrorists who carried out the attack in the Army base were highly trained and vowed to hunt down those behind it.

In a unique initiative, a leading private hospital directed its staff to abstain from shaking hands with each other to avoid spreading of infection.

In an alarming reflection of how bad the law and orders situation in city really is, 20 people were reported missing today itself.

In an announcement which is expected to bring relief to homebuyers, authorities said the process of demarcating eco-sensitive zone around the Bird sanctuary has been cleared.

In an attempt to curb power theft, the government has decided to reward people for providing information on those indulging in electricity thefts.

In an attempt to grow more medicinal plants, the forest department is prepared a list of Ayurvedic practitioners who can provide information about plants with high medicinal value that can be grown in forests.

In an endeavour to light up others' lives through the gesture of 'giving', they carried out an activity wherein woolen clothes, blankest, thermals and eatables were collected from the city and distributed in the park.

In an escalation of the protracted pay disputes, the players decided to boycott the international tour.

In an expansion of the union council of ministers, he was made the finance minister.

In an important decision meant to speed up official work, the cabinet gave more financial rights to senior officers.

In an important ruling, the court said that nursing homes without an intensive care unit facility cannot carry out surgical operations on a patient as absence of ICU posed danger to the patient's life.

In any democratic society, protestors play an important part in the civil, social and political life.

In burn cases, internal organs of patients become stiffer due to lack of blood and oxygen supply and excessive fluid loss.

In colloquial terms, diabetes is about sugar.

In compliance with the directions of the Election Commission, the district administration is making all efforts to ensure a pleasant voting experience for the differently-abled in the district.

In course of talk, he told me this news.

In his first public remarks on the controversial issue, he justified his actions.

In his most significant break with tradition yet, a top religious leader touched and washed the feet of an old man.

In his tenure as state police chief spanning two years, he has taken many initiatives to control crime and curb rising drug menace in the state.

In last two decades various institutes of Mountaineering have gained a lot of expertise and now are planning to add new researches and techniques to prepare highly skilled mountaineers.

In light of the history given, these cases have never been reported to the authorities.

In light of the ongoing events in country, our organization will be making a donation to 'UNICEF'.

In likely relief from rising mercury in the state the Met office predicted thunderstorm and rain activity from today.

In many accidents involving public transport vehicle, it has been noticed that overloading played a major role.

In many parts of the country, several conservation efforts for natural sources are underway.

In my view, the entire matter should be probed by retired judge.

In my whole career, I have always worked for the people.

In nature, no two objects are identical.

In one of his first interactions with media, he spoke about the allegations against him.

In one of the largest anti-encroachment drives held in the recent past, district administration demolished over 500 illegal structures.

In order to add shelf life, manufactures add artificial ingredients to the food.

In order to empower women to protect themselves against any type of aggression and harassment, police launched a month long self-defense training programme.

In order to encourage children and youngsters to excel in academics as well as sports, a social event was organized by the rotary club.

In order to ensure that the children have good future, parents often compromise on their own needs.

In order to score well, it is important that the students have a thorough knowledge about the paper pattern and are able to use it strategically.

In order to sensitize locals on the pressing problem of garbage scattered all around the city, citizen-organization conducted garbage awareness walks.

In order to stop the accused form flying out of the country, police have alerted airports about seven people wanted in the inter-state kidney racket.

In order to strengthen better traffic management, the state traffic directorate procured hundreds of CCTV cameras to be installed at select locations across the state.

In personal as well as professional life, at times it happens that even your closest friends are unable to stand by you.

In separate incidents, two unidentified young men were injured by speeding buses.

In some relief to guest teachers across the state, the court extended the time period of their service in government schools by two more months.

In some relief, the weather department has forecast reduction in rain activity from tomorrow onwards.

In spite of several schemes, under which pipelines and water tanks were constructed by the authorities, there was no respite as most of the water sources have also dried up.

In the absence of mark-sheets, the students could neither apply for jobs nor seek admission elsewhere.

In the day and age that we live in, electricity is the most important aspect of modern living.

In the hilly terrain, farming is one of the most challenging tasks.

In the past 48 hours, light to moderate rain occurred at a few places and heavy showers were recorded at isolated places.

In the past few years we have witnessed difficult times and war.

In the wake of objections raised by the defence authorities, the forest department has decided to discontinue using drones to monitor movement of elephant on the outskirts of the city.

In the wake of recent bomb blasts, police has tightened the security.

In the year gone by, we have been actively involved in operations against our adversaries.

In this era of inflation, we need to financially plan our life.

In times like this, we should unite.

In today's fast-paced world, health is at stake.

In today's modern world when we are depending on technology, all our equipments are based on electricity.

In view of the heavy rains, railways announced partial cancellation of at least ten trains.

In what according to the neighbours was a feud, both side suffered heavy loss of lives.

In what appeared like a plot to derail trains, Pandrol fastening clips were found missing from tracks.

In what can dent the faith of common people in the efficacy of the justice delivery system thousands of cases are pending for many decades in the courts.

In what has come as piece of good news for temporary teachers in various aided schools, the education department is all set to give them an opportunity to apply for getting benefits and pay that their permanent counterparts get.

In what is perhaps the first such instance, a court pressed charges against the officer investigating the case.

In what seems to be a move to strengthen the relationship, they visited each other's house.

In what would be a further blow for president, three cabinet ministers have resigned.

In yet another addition to the recent spate of burglaries, burglars struck a house in a posh colony.

ADDITIONAL EXAMPLES:

In a 300-page judgement in the 20-year-old case, the apex court ordered that . . .

In a bid to demoralize the enemies . . .

In a bid to ensure safety and security of students commuting by school buses . . .

In a bid to exercise control and ensure smooth operation . . .

In a bid to motivate security personnel . . .

In a bid to revive the fortunes of the . . .

In a big relief to homebuyers . . .

In a bitter twist to the tragedy . . .

In a boost to health facilities . . .

In a boost to promote industrialization and attract investors . . .

In a boost to scam probe . . .

In a breather for the accused . . .

In a clear signal to opposition . . .

In a cruel irony of fate . . .

In a daring daytime robbery . . .

In a decision that may have far-reaching implications . . .

In a decision which would help students . . .

In a departure from the usual . . .

In a disturbing incident . . .

In a dramatic turn of events . . .

In a fast-paced, dramatic turn of events …

In a first of its kind study . . .

In a grim reminder of the hit and run case . . .

In a macabre incident . . .

In a major jolt to the . . .

In a major terror strike . . .

In a morale booster for company . . .

In a move aimed at improving soil health . . .

In a move compliant with court direction . . .

In a much anticipated moment . . .

In a new twist in the case . . .

In a quiet move . . .

In a record of its sorts . . .

In a reflection of what grit and determination can achieve . . .

In a sad reminder of the village incident . . .

In a sensational disclosure . . .

In a series of moves . . .

In a setback to medical association . . .

In a shocking incident . . .

In a show of strong protest . . .

In a spine-chilling incident of honour killing . . .

In a stark reversal of previous reports . . .

In a statement, the media company said . . .

In a story both heart-wrenching and warming,

In a surprise move . . .

In a surprising development, he has now claimed that . . .

In a unique initiative . . .

In a victory speech at his office . . .

In a video of a public meeting that appears to have gone viral . . .

In a world first . . .

In addition . . .

In an attempt of dig out the truth . . .

In an attempt to maintain peace and harmony . . .

In an interesting finding announced at the meeting . . .

In an order that would speed up construction work of metro rail . . .

In an unexpected twist to the . . .

In an unprecedented move (step) . . .

In another instance of people taking the law into their hands . . .

In another related (interesting) development . . .

In any case (event) . . .

In brief . . .

In comparison . . .

In conclusion . . .

In contrast (to) . . .

In earlier . . .

In essence . . .

In final analysis . . .

In final consideration . . .

In fresh troubles for the agitators . . .

In general . . .

In good news for tourists and wildlife enthusiasts . . .

In haste to flee . . .

In her petition at the court, he asked the court to give permission . . .

In his opening remarks at the joint media interaction . . .

In his welcome address,

In its report to be released tomorrow . . .

In keeping with the tradition (trend) . . .

In like fashion . . .

In my opinion . . .

In near simultaneous attacks across neighbouring states . . .

In one of the most sweeping use of his presidential powers . . .

In order to ensure grievances of people . . .

In other words . . .

In particular . . .

In perhaps the first instance of its kind . . .

In protest against such incidents ....

In reference to the conversation . . .

In response to a question . . .

In second such incident in the fortnight . . .

In short . . .

In summary . . .

In the backdrop of a bitter rivalry . . .

In the day and age of Internet . . .

In the days after the raid that injured him . . .

In the event of a change of environment . . .

In the face of life threatening adversity . . .

In the final analysis . . .

In the first of its kind event . . .

In the first place . . .

In the larger interest of the people . . .

In the light of all-round criticism . . .

In the long run . . .

In the meantime . . .

In the midst of . . .

In the past . . .

In the same way . . .

In the second such incident in two days . . .

In the second such judgement in three weeks . . .

In the true sense of the word . . .

In this case . . .

In this situation . . .

In turn . . .

In two minds over whether to ignore the call . . .

In view of this . . .

In what appears to be the violation of ceasefire . . .

In what believed to be a respite to old man . . .

In what can bring respite to them . . .

In what is being viewed as a clear case of . . .

In what is suspected to be a case of . . .

In yet another incident affecting cross-border relations between . . .

In yet another instance of . . .

How to Start a Sentence -- Using 'WITH'

With 12 people rescued, we still have 8 missing.

With 20 of its buses broken down, the STC didn't operate services on Tuesday.

With a deafening roar, they charged at the culprits.

With a rise in violent activities across the globe, it has become very important to spread awareness about non-violence among the masses.

With a variety of fields to choose from, students are keen to grab a professional course certificate in their area of choice.

With all the teams at the World Cup having played at least one match each, it's time to take stock of the initial performance.

With both kidneys damaged, he has to regularly undergo dialysis.

With businesses going increasingly digital, it has also become important for the customers to be smart in their approaches.

With changing time and busy schedule, parents are not able to give the amount of time they use to get from their parents.

With direct involvement from the officials, they are hoping to improve the quality of education given in their schools.

With doctors on strike, the emergency services have been left in the hands of para-medical staff.

With early marriage comes early parenting as well.

With elections round the corner, talk of caste has heated up.

With entire world getting modernized, means of communication have taken a new form as well.

With festival only a week away, families are busy shopping new items.

With flickering light of a lantern in their backdrop, a group of villagers huddled together to listen to news on a radio.

With four babies dying after being administered vaccine, a wave of panic has spread across the state.

With help from the government we are able to renovate our houses.

With her achievements, Mary has put us on the global map.

With increased temperature, the power situation is worsening.

With increasing human population, there is a pressure on the lands for accommodation.

With incredible bad luck, bullet lodged in his chest.

With inflationary pressure mounting, the government is looking at further import duty cuts.

With investigations into the scandal picking pace, many new facts are emerging.

With many hospitals suffering from acute shortage of doctors, quacks are playing with the lives of thousands of patients daily.

With marshals now posted at the "no park sign", no cars can be parked there any longer.

With maximum temperature crossing the 40 degree Celsius mark, the water level in the river has gone down.

With moist eyes, scores of people bid their final adieu to slain police officer.

With more than 100 snakes spotted in their locality in the past one year, residents decided quite some time back that they needed to develop skills of their own to deal with the reptiles.

With New Year only a few days away, we have several plans in our mind.

With no blankets or enough woolen clothes to fight off the chill, those on the streets were seen lighting fires with scraps found on the roads.

With no income at all, they had to struggle to make both ends meet.

With no means to sustain himself, he tried to commit suicide.

With no respite from the intense heat, locals are preferring to stay indoors.

With no untoward incident, the situation, as of now, was reported to be fine.

With over 30 years of experience in literature, she is confident of winning the award.

With passage of time, he forgot all the sufferings.

With rapid advances in information technology, data is an asset whose value keeps increasing over time.

With sanitation workers on strike, we are sure to face the garbage disposal problems.

With so many matches, the players may find it tough to cope with the pressure.

With stray animals routinely entering farmlands and destroy standing crops, farmers have been forced to take extreme measure like fencing their fields with electric wires.

With summer just having started, many parts of the city were facing power cuts.

With support from the nationalists, he gained a majority.

With tears in my eyes, I started reliving the various memories I had of her.

With the beginning of December, most of the schools start conducting pre-board examination.

With the elections having concluded it s now time for everyone to work for development of the country.

With the examination season round the corner, many students fall prey to stress.

With the fresh inductions, the strength of the Union ministry has gone up to 50.

With the health of the PM deteriorating, party leaders met apparently to chalk out the next course of action.

With the help of spiritual teachings, we can guide students towards a better life.

With the kind of mandate she received, President is expected to reform the policies.

With the onset of summer, many people are having a hard time grappling with severe water crisis.

With the onset of summers, the days have become longer and brighter.

With the onset of winter and the season's first fog spell, airline and train services have taken a hit.

With the philosophy to always dream big, and achieve the impossible, failure is something that is inevitable.

With the proliferation of e-devices, more and more people are communicating through digital modes.

With the roof leaking and dumps all around, it is not at all easy to stay here.

With the scenario so distressing for most areas, how was it that sec-20 got water supply with most parameters normal?

With the world cup two years away, players have ample time.

With this, we all froze in our spots.

With three main roads closed, there will be additional pressure on other roads.

With time, festival has changed.

With transformer out of service, residents have not received power for the last three days.

With uncertainty over government formation prevalent for nearly a month, governor has stepped in to end it.

With very little winter rain this time around, most of the water sources have also depleted drastically.

With waters reaching the knee, residents had to rush to safety.

With wing spans up to a yard and intimidating sharp claws, those birds were really awful.

Without active and regular citizen engagement, no change can occur.

Without knowing ourselves, we will get nowhere.

Without support from you, I wouldn't be doing as well as I am right now.

Without wealth, life can become fraught with problems.

ADDITIONAL EXAMPLES:

With a beaming smile on her face, she said . . .

With a deep sense of anguish, we announce . . .

With a flag fluttering atop . . .

With a low voice, he said to his wife . . .

With a vision of creating employability and a life-saving workforce . . .

With all eyes on him . . .

With almost everything going his way right from winning the toss . . .

With an aim to drawing more tourists . . .

With an eye on her wealth . . .

With an eye on the imminent midterm poll . . .

With an intense cold wave sweeping . . .

With deadly quake raising questions over safety of nuclear reactors worldwide . . .

With differing interpretations coming out of his statement . . .

With due promptitude . . .

With economic growth slowing down . . .

With electricity becoming a recurring problem . . .

With hunting banned in reserve forest area . . .

With Independence Day nearing . . .

With instances of tigers invading into human habitat . . .

With just 10 days left for . . .

With just a week to go for exams . . .

With less than three weeks before the . . .

With militancy petering out . . .

With mystery behind the missing ship deepening . . .

With no help from his friends, whom he had approached as soon as . . .

With no knowledge about . . .

With no specific reference to . . .

With poll date approaching and electioneering picking up . . .

With regard to the treatment meted out to him . . .

With several incidents of thefts coming to light . . .

With situation slipping out of control . . .

With so much emphasis being put on staying thin . . .

With survey getting over on Wednesday . . .

With the amendment . . .

With the announcement of the . . .

With the average age of a girl at marriage being 18 years . . .

With the captain having its lips sealed . . .

With the curtain coming down on . . .

With the ultimatum expiring on Monday . . .

With the winter just starting out . . .

With the workplace smoking ban deadline two weeks away . . .

With this in mind . . .

With two years to go for elections . . .

With uncertainty surrounding the schedule . . .

Within days of issuing strict refund laws . . .

How to Start a Sentence -- Using 'QUESTION WORDS'

What followed then was a series of nightmares.

What had driven the court to appoint a committee was the absence of any regulation to deal with such types of cases.

What marked vice chancellor from his famous contemporaries such as x, y, z was his simplicity.

What may work in the US may not be applicable elsewhere.

What was the forecast to happen in the long term two years ago appears imminent now.

What we have lost can't be brought back.

What we have warned of has finally come to pass.

What we thought was a successful event has taken a sad turn.

Whatever be the reasons, one celebrates having had a safe festival.

Whatever food we had fled with, is finished.

Whatever the context, making such statements is uncalled for.

Whatever you become in your life, first become a good human being.

When he gets blacked out, he hooks on to new technology to reach out to people.

When I met him a month ago, he was in a jovial mood.

When I requested him to identify himself, he started misbehaving.

When I step on playground, I am not thinking that a Russian never did this or a Russian never did that.

When introduced into the navy, it will be our largest warship.

When it came to crime, national capital was not far behind any other state.

When people reach heights; they tend to get a bit egoistic.

When project comes through, it will spell the end of the long period of neglect city.

When quake struck, panicked residents ran out of their houses and were seen hanging outside in anticipation of aftershocks.

When she headed for the roof, he was stopped by unknown person.

When she is with her family, she makes it a point to keep all gadgets and communication devices away.

When there has been a problem of this nature, citizens of the county have had to pay.

When things seem difficult, take it as an opportunity to learn a lesson.

When you face difficulty, you should tell yourself there is some good at the end of it.

When you understand the tactics and strategy of your opponents, it is easier to contest.

Whenever exams approach, many students start panicking.

Whenever there has been a problem, we have stood together.

Whichever road we may take, we shall be late.

Why it is just what you had done all these years.

ADDITIONAL EXAMPLES:

What is of concern is . . .

What is worrying him most is that the . . .

What made me who I am is the sum of all . . .

Whatever the claims may be . . .

When contacted, the AD who had escorted the team told that . . .

When finished, the space station will be . . .

When I was their age . . .

When it comes to how women are treated . . .

How to Start a Sentence -- Using 'ING' FORM of VERBS

Acing the exams is not a tough job, provided one is ready to invest time and effort in studies right from day one.

Acknowledging importance and contribution of poetry to world literature, UNESCO declared March 21 as World Poetry Day in 1999.

Acknowledging that the work is very complex, the investigating team said that there is no timeline to complete the investigation.

Acknowledging that there will be some minor problems when a massive change takes place, he said that things will smoothen in the times to come.

Acting tough, Information Commission directed transfer of the two senior officers.

Addressing the inaugural session of the day-long event,

Admitting the petitions of accused, judge posted the matter for hearing on Aug 16.

Answering a question regarding the situation along the international border, Army General said, "It will be alright."

Apprehending arrest, he fled to Malaysia.

Asserting that the basic fundamentals of economy were sound and healthy, the PM said the government has been taking all measures to correct imbalances on the macro front.

Assuming that the tiger was alive, villagers fled from the spot.

Attaining the age of majority in an individual's life has its own significance.

Avoiding water from accumulating and covering stored water are the best precautions to prevent diseases caused by mosquitoes.

Barring isolated shops, majority of markets and schools remained open in and around the town.

Barring reports of election slips being snatched at some places, polling was peaceful.

Barring two incidents of clashes, the polling was held peacefully in all the districts.

Battling heavy rains, rescue teams evacuated thousands of people who were stranded in remote corners of the state.

Being a financial services company, you have to make sure that you have a comprehensive policy on cyber security.

Being a marketer, he travels a lot.

Being a single parent can be challenging.

Being a woman, it was a challenge to establish myself in public life.

Being made in compliance with the orders of the court, medical facility was to be completed by 2016.

Being named the tallest man has meant very little for him.

Being old does not mean that we cannot learn new things.

Being open to technologies of the future doesn't mean we have to accept all their uses.

Being perishable items, horticulture produce needs extra attention during storage and transportation.

Being raised with women, I saw their side of things.

Being scared of the outcome of all our work may result in complete inactivity.

Being seriously overweight can nearly double a person's chances of suffering migraines.

Being the custodian of the Constitution, President has to maintain the dignity of his post.

Being the only people in a movie theatre made me feel good.

Being the second largest populated country in the world, India is one of the largest markets for retail and service industries.

Braving the summer heat and dust, hundreds of contestants raced against time to reach voters for their valuable ballot.

Breaking his silence over the factional feud in the committee, he said there can be no division in the committee till he is there.

Breaking his silence, he declared he had nothing to do with the contentious issue.

Bringing about security is dependent on many factors.

Brushing aside charges of nepotism on including a father son duo in the bill drafting committee, he said it was question of experience, rather than individuals.

Budgeting is an effective way to reduce unnecessary spending.

Burning of coal is the main source of air pollution, a fallout of increasing urbanization and industrialization.

Burning of dry leaves adds to pollution woes.

Burning of fossil fuels emit gases, which are responsible for air pollution and global warming.

Buying things from online shopping websltes is hugely popular nowadays.

Chairing a high-level meeting comprising officials of the Railway Board, railway minister carried out a comprehensive review of the safety measures for the entire railway network.

Choosing mutual funds for investment reduce the risk.

Claiming 'vital' leads in the serial blasts, police has detained two terrorists.

Coming as a huge relieve for parents. a 6-year-old boy was rescued successfully.

Coming in to his help, district magistrate has announced compensation.

Commenting on the uproar that his film has triggered, the actor said, "It's appalling."

Complaining about little things isn't worth your time.

Complaining of heavy power cuts, entrepreneurs at industrial estate claimed that they have lost 10% of their manufacturing capacity due to random load shedding.

Condemning the police attitude, he said the police were trying to scuttle the matter instead of doing their job.

Conserving fuel is not just a matter of one day but a lifestyle.

Considering that he was top administrator earlier, it is sad to see what has happened to him.

Continuing with his brilliant performance in the international games, he won three more medals.

Counting of votes will be held tomorrow.

Covering heritage structures with aluminum panels mean covering the history.

Creating an atmosphere of fear is not the correct way to deal with the crime.

Creating jobs for the youth should be the key focus areas for the government.

Curbing depletion of ozone layer is need of the hour.

Debating against the provision, opposition contended that it will make situation grim.

Delivering his speech at the annual investiture ceremony of the police force, chief guest said the officials should always be particular about their uniform as it set the symbol of their pride and status.

Differing with the remarks of his minister crediting himself with division of the neighbouring country, president said we never interfered in internal matters of any country.

Discussing the importance of reading, she says, "Books are a great way to tone the mind."

Dismissing any news on discord in the rank, party chief sounded confident of everything falling in line.

Dismissing charges of being an opportunist and of betraying him, she said he did not keep its word about putting on hold contentious issue.

Dismissing the plea to refrain from buying gold for the next few months, women are giving into the lure of the yellow metal.

Doing away with myths, science has maintained that leprosy is neither infectious nor contagious.

Donating organs is one of the most humane ways to save lives.

Dubbing the hiked power tariff as unjustified, a city resident said, "There is no improvement in power infrastructure".

During peak summer, demand for water increases and this leads to water scarcity.

Eating a healthy diet is one of the most important elements to do away with fatigue.

Eating healthy and nutritious food is crucial for the children.

Eating homemade and nutritious food at proper intervals keeps us fit.

Elaborating on the preparations to tackle the floods, commissioner said. "All concerned departments are working hard to keep the situation under control."

Eliminating malaria is both possible and necessary.

Eliminating terrorism is among the top-most priorities for us.

Encouraging women to stay healthy, a hospital conducted health camps exclusively for women.

Enforcing discipline over the unauthorized use of mobile phones along forward areas or sensitive establishments is a cause of concern for the Army.

Ensuring a healthy society is the first step towards realizing the dream of a developed nation.

Enunciating the drawbacks of technology, a child psychologist says, it has driven people apart.

Exercising more than your potential can make you feel tired and lazy.

Failing to impart education as per the law is equal to not letting students avail of their rights.

Fearing for his life, he tried contacting the helpline number.

Fearing rise in poaching activities around New Year, an alert has been issued in Tiger Reserve.

Finding the abode that keeps us comfortable and safe is important.

Flying objects coming in contacts with an airplane is hazard.

Following any practices or actions blindly is work of a fool.

Following complaints of leopard sightings by residents of the villages, camera traps have been installed in forest area to ascertain leopard presence.

Following heavy rainfall alert by the meteorological department, the administration ordered all schools to remain closed today.

Following Metro success in the national capital, several states have been demanding similar networks in their own cities.

Following relaxation of curfew, people rushed out in large numbers.

Following the downpour, which crippled normal life in some parts of the city, administration has declared a holiday for educational institutions.

Getting a university education remains a dream for many youths.

Getting enough quality sleep can help protect your mental and physical health as well as quality of life.

Getting piped water continues to be a pipe dream for millions of people.

Getting to the truth may not be easy.

Getting wind of her return, he sweet-talked to her.

Giving a fresh impetus to the education sector, the government launched an online portal to curb teacher absenteeism in the primary and secondary schools.

Giving an insight into his childhood, he says by 12th grade his dream was to play football for his hometown and eventually work for a bank.

Giving money the right value means neither exaggerating nor underestimating its worth.

Giving wings to your dream, the fair has various companies under one roof.

Going by past records, one remains unsure if anyone will be held accountable.

Going by the condition of the carcass, it appeared that it was one month old.

Going by the importance of the case, it was transferred to an ACP-level officer.

Going through records running into thousands of pages would take time.

Grabbing the opportunities, he stole valuables.

Grappling with mobile call drop menace, telecom operators committed to install 25 thousand towers within a year.

Hardening its stand against the government, opposition ruled out any cooperation with them.

Having gone without a single drop of rain for about six months, we got some rain yesterday.

Having occurred due to the discharge of poisonous chemical gas in 1984, Bhopal Gas Tragedy is considered as one of the horrendous incidents that shook the world.

Having old parents and being the only earning member of the family, he has planned his finances well.

Having saved money, we went on a foreign trip.

Having seen struggle and hardships from close quarters, she wanted to help those who are economically backwards.

Hearing people shout, elephant ran away.

Highlighting his good work and clean image as a senior officer, he said, "From the first day I entered office, I have been adhering to zero tolerance to corruption and has not done anything wrong in dispensing the responsibility.

Highlighting the issues concerning women, he said two things that should receive renewed focus are gender equality and safety of women.

Holding your head above and flapping your hands and feet, you remain afloat.

Hosting and caring for elderly people comes with its sets of problems.

Hurling stones and setting public property on fire, the agitators went on the rampage in the town.

Incorporating certain foods in your diet, like citrus fruits, eggs, whole grain foods and seafood, can help improve your immunity.

Indicating that it was in no mood to relent, the administration warned the culprits of stringent actions.

Installing a GPS device in the car is helpful because we are directed towards where to search for it if it gets stolen.

Intensifying its drive against unauthorized construction in the city, the municipal corporation sealed and demolished 20 residential properties.

Interacting with officers during a video conference, CM said strict action should be taken against anyone found guilty of mischievous activities.

Judging students on the basis of marks, we label students as weak or intelligent.

Keeping aside all other issues, we are just demanding our money back.

Keeping government records as a personal property is a criminal offence.

Keeping in mind a risk of obesity, Health Ministry has issued a fresh set of guidelines.

Keeping in mind the damage heavy rains may cause, Power Corporation has started setting up rain-resistant poles.

Keeping in mind the upcoming election, district administration is all set to educate people on how to use their franchise.

Keeping in view the sentiments of public at large, it was decided to transfer the investigation to the central investigation agency.

Keeping in view the situation prevailing there, it was necessary to impose restrictions on entry into the area.

Keeping low internet penetration and poor internet connectivity in mind, the app had been designed to work offline also.

Keeping your cool during stressful situations is crucial for problem-solving.

Leading a healthy lifestyle can go a long way in preventing the onset of any disease, including cancer.

Learning happens when one is free to observe.

Learning new skills and acquiring new knowledge are vital these days.

Leaving stray incidents of arguments, the protest passed away peacefully.

Linking the intense heat wave and drought to environmental degradation, PM made a strong pitch for a mass movement to save forests and conserve "every drop" of water during the upcoming rainy season.

Living a nine-to-five desk life can be demanding on health and wellness.

Living a virtuous, upright life is a challenge.

Looking at the mangled car, one can imagine the speed at which the vehicle was being driven.

Looking for online discounts on all sorts of merchandise, people are using the e-platform for their shopping.

Lying by the bed dying man were suicide notes.

Maintaining a balance diet for all of us is very important.

Maintaining a healthy lifestyle is important.

Maintaining greenery and cleanliness should be a never-ending process.

Maintaining that he is not a businessman but a social entrepreneur, he said most of the allegations levelled against him have not been proved yet.

Making a time table is a good thing to work in an organized manner.

Making the end of spring season, summer heat has finally arrived.

Managing office and home simultaneously is an arduous task.

Managing the disease is possible with the right lifestyle choices.

Mapping and **monitoring** of glaciers can provide answers to how climate change is affecting the glaciers.

Mastering your mind is different from controlling or suppressing it.

Mounting a fresh attack, student leaders accused the administration of stifling voices of dissent of students across the country.

Moving a writ petition, he sought protection of his life.

Moving out of the traditional realm, women are now establishing themselves as efficacious entrepreneurs.

Negotiating is an important aspect of everybody's life.

Observing that bad infrastructure and a dearth of good quality education in schools are the primary reasons for migration from the hills, court imposed restraints on the purchase of luxury goods for officials.

Opening a bank account has now become an easy task.

Owing to prevailing chaos and misinformation at the railway station, many have cancelled their holiday plans.

Owning a vehicle means easy and instant availability of transport.

Paying excessive attention on body's shape and looks has become a trend.

Peering through the net, one of the boy told journalists what it was like inside that bus.

Planning is the key to prepare for any competitive exam.

Playing at the international level means you have to be in the best shape possible.

Postponing a task only adds to your stress.

Presenting the budget in the assembly, finance ministers said the budget is 10% higher than last fiscal's.

Preventing children from doing what they like and forcing them to concentrate only on studies is not helpful.

Projecting confidence doesn't come easily to everyone.

Providing good facilities to all employees within an affordable price range is both challenging and motivating.

Pushing the party's election campaign into high gear, a top leader said he will never sell the country.

Putting a smile on someone's face can make you happy.

Putting the doctor-patient relationship to disgrace, doctor removed the kidney of the patient to sell it for money.

Quitting smoking is hard but it is not as hard as going through the multiple health issues it can bring to you.

Raising drug abuse among the youth is a pressing problem.

Realizing the importance of humour, kings and emperors used to keep jesters in their courts.

Realizing where he is, Simon fled.

Recognizing and applauding all those who are doing a good job is an essential feature of an evolving society.

Recycling products made of paper, plastic and glass can be the best way to conserve the environment.

Reeling under acute staff crunch, the police department assigned the task of tackling traffic to trainee policewomen.

Remembering the minutes before the accident, survivors claimed that all the passengers were in good mood.

Replacing oils containing high transfats with healthier options will have no impact on the taste of food.

Riding on sympathy wave, she won the assembly seat.

Ruling out any exemption from toll collection at national highways, road minister said that if people want good services they will have pay for that.

Running is one of the best forms of exercise.

Saving money has not only been the crucial need of people, but also an expression of maturity.

Saying sorry is not the only way to apologize.

Seeking to preserve buildings and sites of historic, aesthetic, cultural or environment values, the government is planning to bring a special legislation to cover unprotected heritage in the state.

Selecting the right mentors is more important than you might imagine.

Sensing danger, he tried to escape.

Sensing danger, office staff quickly locked themselves up inside the office premises.

Sensing trouble, he accelerated his bike.

Shaking his head in disbelief, he said, "It shows how selfish they are."

Sharing love and laughter is always a good thing.

Shifting to a new system takes time.

Showing solidarity with workers on Labor Day, President signed an executive order requiring paid sick leave for employees of federal contractors.

Sighting increased levels of pollution, the government had banned diesel-run vehicles on the road.

Sipping some strong black coffee, we watched the football match.

Sitting around a rectangular table with a select group of global news agency editors, President took questions one by one on subjects of wider global concerns.

Sitting on a beach, I was watching the sun setting on a sea that was slowly turning from blue-green to deep indigo.

Smelling danger, robbers attacked the security personnel.

Standing 390 meter high when completed, this minaret will be five time as high as Qutub Minar.

Standing united, the whole country should protest against racism.

Starting Dec 20, 2016, he wrote to me about 10 letters.

Stating that freedom of expression is welcome, he said, "Let debate go on."

Stating that the country will plunge into anarchy in absence of Constitutional sovereignty, a judged said it is mandatory for all to abide by the rules of the law.

Stating that there is a need to fuel skill training and workforce development, President's daughter said it is necessary to align what is being taught in the classroom with economic realities.

Staying alert is a pre-requisite of driving a vehicle in the hilly areas.

Staying alone at night is scary.

Staying fit is important, but lacking necessary nutrients in your diet to look slim is bad idea.

Staying in the Antarctica where the minimum temperature goes up to -90 degrees Celsius is really a challenge.

Staying physically fit and healthy is imperative for leading a good life.

Stocking up on a wide variety of designs is must for jewelers.

Striking in a big way, militant killed 100 people.

Struggling to cope with the industry's growing reliance on automation, young techies are turning to psychologist to deal with the rising anxiety and stress.

Summing up the proposed industrial policy, principal secretary of village industries board said that almost all benefits that a big unit is entitle to get under new policy, would be given to small units also.

Suspecting procedural discrepancies while offering free education to poor children in private schools, the finance department instructed the education department to carry out a fresh check of beneficiaries.

Suspecting the formation of a new lake in the glacier region after a recent heavy landslide, a specialized team was asked to proceed to the region.

Swooping down on various locations, investigating agency with the help of local police apprehended five people for their involvement in the blasts.

Taking a break from work, I step out for a lunch with my colleague.

Taking children out amidst nature helps them in learning things which are not possible indoors.

Taking cognizance of traffic problems, traffic police formed a plan to allow one-way traffic on several routes of the town to tackle traffic snarls.

Taking into account the troubles faced by people in obtaining and renewal of driving licenses, transport minister started additional transport offices.

Taking part in physical activities not only make children active and healthy, but also stimulate the development of their social and communication skills.

Taking serious note of the severe air pollution in the state, the National Human Rights Commission slammed the authorities for not taking steps through the year to control the hazard.

Talking about the facilities and infrastructures for sports in India, he said, "A lot of improvement is needed."

Talking to reporters after a meeting of the party parliamentary board, party leader said the party was now in election mode.

Terming it a personal matter, he denied interacting with the media.

Throwing light on the kind of furniture in trend these days, an owner of a furniture shop said,

Tightening the reins on the administration, aviation minster announced a series of measures to passenger safety.

Towering on both sides of the highway, those mountains look appalling.

Trying to dictate what people should consume is taking away their right of choice and an affront to their basic human right.

Trying to take a selfie atop a fort proved fatal for a youth as he fell from there and died.

Untangling your life is the key to success, happiness and looking radiant.

Urging people not to fall prey to rumour-mongers, police commissioner denied imposition of prohibitory orders anywhere in the city.

Urging the crowd to respond, he asked them whether they were 'culprits' to which the chorus said 'no'.

Using phones while driving claim hundreds of lives every year.

Waiting nearby on the Indian side were family members of 54 prisoner of War.

Walking fast for about 35 minutes a day and five times a week helps in improving symptoms of mild to moderate depression.

Winning the toss was like crossing the first hurdle at the VCA ground.

Wondering who would burst firecrackers outside here, I walked towards the window.

Wondering whom to blame for this condition, I turned to myself.

Wrapping up the trial of the acid attack case, the sessions court sentenced the accused to 10 years rigorous imprisonment.

ADDITIONAL EXAMPLES:

Acknowledging the gravity of the issue . . .

Acting on the tip off . . .

Adding a new twist to an already bizarre tale . . .

Admitting that there is a shortage of personnel in the army, a senior army officer said . . .

Adopting a non-negotiable approach to protect homebuyers, the court said . . .

Aiming to provide faster and cheaper connectivity to passengers . . .

Amending its order that had been in force for a little over a year . . .

Appearing for the pilots . . .

Arguing her own case . . .

Asserting that indiscipline would not be tolerated in the college, VC said . . .

Being carried by his custodian,

Being out of practice . . .

Bracing for still more foul weather . . .

Braving heavy rains . . .

Braving hostile winds and snow . . .

Braving the cold and dark . . .

Breaking off from tradition to . . .

Brushing aside the plea/report . . .

Calling it a mistake . . .

Calling it a terror strike . . .

Carrying the body of the victim . . .

Challenging the validity of . . .

Citing a data . . .

Citing difficulties faced by the students . . .

Citing social engagements . . .

Citing the exemption clause . . .

Claiming that it was a fake encounter . . .

Clarifying that . . .

Clutching hard her 5-year old son . . .

Coming back to the point . . .

Coming down heavily on the moves by the officers . . .

Coming heavily under fire for her alleged comments . . .

Commending the contribution of the army in peace missions, the army chief said . . .

Commenting on the incident . . .

Complaining about the food quality at training academics, players said . . .

Complying with a special court's order . . .

Concealing himself to catch the thief . . .

Confirming the incident/move . . .

Considering the matter . . .

Considering the seriousness of the issue . . .

Considering the unfavourable weather conditions . . .

Countering his claim . . .

Cracking down on sale of tobacco . . .

Cutting across party lines . . .

Cutting past the language barriers . . .

Delivering her address . . .

Depending on the situation . . .

Detailing the ordeal he went through while working as . . .

Devoting an entire page on the agitation . . .

Disclosing that to News Channel, officers said . . .

Discussing the present state of affairs . . .

Dismissing concerns over the shortages . . .

Disposing a petition filed by 50-year old . . .

Disposing of a batch of petitions . . .

Drawing attention to how considerable academic time was getting lost due to . . .

Easing the situation . . .

Echoing his sentiment/views, another student said . . .

Elaborating further on it . . .

Elaborating on her plan, she said . . .

Elaborating on his decision to abstain from drugs, he said . . .

Elaborating on the way virtual currencies are traded, a trader said . . .

Elaborating, he added that . . .

Emerging from the shadow . . .

Enumerating the decisions "to be implemented soon" . . .

Enumerating the decisions taken by them for the welfare of the people, he said . . .

Explaining how the budget has given the much-needed push to sugar sector, he said . . .

Explaining the significance of the satellite phones, she said . . .

Expressing concern, spokesman said . . .

Expressing determination to build 'good relation' with neighbour country . . .

Expressing disappointment over the cancellation of meeting . . .

Expressing satisfaction over the order, he said . . .

Eyeing an entry into the Guinness book . . .

Fearing exposure . . .

Following a court's directive . . .

Giving a call for unity between Muslims and Christians . . .

Giving a chronological account of the events leading to . . .

Giving a new twist to the story . . .

Giving advisory to people to avoid heatstroke, a medical officer said . . .

Giving back on its stand . . .

Giving credits to his parents for his success, he said . . .

Giving details about the events that preceded the faceoff between two armies, the sources said . . .

Giving details of how he survived the night in the forest which is known to have wild bears, he said . . .

Giving its nod in principle, the committee has decided . . .

Giving them an escape route . . .

Going by day one of the campaign, it seems . . .

Going by the condition of her house, it is certain that . . .

Hardening its stand on the policy . . .

Hearing a litigation . . .

Highlighting the challenge to manage . . .

Highlighting the key features of the scheme . . .

Highlighting the poor state of schools . . .

Hinting for the first time that . . .

Hitting back at his predecessor . . .

Hitting out at the committee . . .

Hoisting the National Flag . . .

Holding a road-show in support of party candidate . . .

Holding placards that said 'no roads, no votes' . . .

Holding the commissioner responsible for the police not complying with the court order . . .

Hoping to cash in on the festival spending spree . . .

Hoping to garner support of various communities . . .

Identifying the website as xyz.com, he said . . .

Ignoring a brutal crackdown that has already claimed a dozen lives . . .

Informing about the proposals submitted in the varsity . . .

Injecting a new twist to the ongoing political drama ...

Interacting with media persons, he said . . .

Keeping in view the situation . . .

Lashing out at his rationale . . .

Launching a blistering attack . . .

Laying emphasis on industrialization . . .

Laying emphasis on the wide range of development work that they had executed, they said . . .

Lending strength to the argument . . .

Likening himself to a referee in a football, he said . . .

Listing out the steps taken to . . .

Listing out the steps that are needed urgently . . .

Living up to one of its promises . . .

Lulling their victim into security . . .

Maintaining that army played an important role . . .

Maintaining the trend . . .

Making a fervent appeal to all citizens to maintain . . .

Making the announcement at a press conference . . .

Marking significant progress in the fight against malaria . . .

Moving the Finance Bill for consideration in Parliament . . .

Moving there does not always mean that . . .

Narrating her woes . . .

Narrating the incident to the media, he said . . .

Noting that the process has created a good atmosphere . . .

Observing that a prima facie . . .

Offering an insight into the way they treat their ailments . . .

Overshooting a signal . . .

Overturning its previous order, the HC disposed the plea of . . .

Passing a slew of directions, the bench said . . .

Passing the orders . . .

Paying tribute to the martyrs . . .

Piercing together the sequence of events . . .

Pointing out that . . .

Praising the works and contribution of former president towards abolishing social discrimination, he said . . .

Pressing for custodial interrogation . . .

Providing details, he said . . .

Putting his foot in the living room . . .

Putting their past firmly behind . . .

Putting to shape the announcement of forming special team . . .

Quoting statistics of . . .

Reacting quickly to calm any panic, the WHO said . . .

Reacting to a news report in a news portal . . .

Reacting to his remark, she said . . .

Reacting to his statement . . .

Reacting to the incident . . .

Reading out the judgement, he said . . .

Realizing the danger he was in . . .

Recalling his days in the office . . .

Recounting the experience so far . . .

Recounting the hardships faced by villagers during rainy days, a villager said . . .

Recounting the harrowing final moments . . .

Recounting the sequence of events . . .

Reeling under a long spell·of intense heat wave . . .

Referring to his off repeated accusations . . .

Referring to migration of tribal . . .

Referring to the law and order situation . . .

Regretting the loss of lives . . .

Rejecting a plea seeking ban on . . .

Remembering how travellers to Boida had been . . .

Replying to a question at a book release function . . .

Replying to the charge . . .

Reserving its final order for May 15 on the probe demand . . .

Respecting the sentiments of the worshippers . . .

Responding to a question about his planes on leaving job, he smiled and said . . .

Responding to a question on how he rated the Budget . . .

Rolling up its sleeves . . .

Rubbishing such allegations . . .

Scrolling through my phone on the way to the office, I stumbled on the news that . . .

Seeking his recall . . .

Seeking to end the row over the land . . .

Seeking to set at rest all doubts . . .

Seeking to vacate the stay . . .

Sensing growing opposition . . .

Sensing the imminent rise in the conflict . . .

Setting a precedent of sorts . . .

Sharing his experience . . .

Sharing his experience while buying fridge for his new home, she said . . .

Sharing his views on pollution, a teacher said . . .

Sharpening its politics prowess . . .

Shedding light on her first book . . .

Showing grit and resilience . . .

Showing serious concerns for rights of orphaned children . . .

Showing their solidarity . . .

Simplifying the process of land acquisition for setting up industries . . .

Sitting at a corner all by himself . . .

Slamming the perpetrators . . .

Softening its stance . . .

Speaking at a joint press conference . . .

Speaking on the role of IT in the development . . .

Speaking on the sidelines of the conference on cyber crime . . .

Speaking on visa on accident scheme . . .

Speaking through a translator . . .

Spelling more trouble for him . . .

Spinning the same story for procuring mobiles . . .

Starting its willingness to cooperate with the . . .

Stepping beyond the position he had so far followed on the issue . . .

Stepping off the bus . . .

Stepping up its attack on the two-month old committee . . .

Stepping up its offensive against the rivals . . .

Stressing on the safety of passenger, a 16-year-old student said . . .

Stressing that all necessary security arrangements have been put in place, the top officer urged to people . . .

Stressing that women have a special role in the society . . .

Striking hard at the societal tendency to impose restrictions on girls with regard to their choice of . . .

Sunning himself on his roof . . .

Suspecting it to be a case of homicide . . .

Sweeping aside the prediction . . .

Taking a grim view of allegation levelled in single-page typed letter . . .

Taking a lead ahead of rivals . . .

Taking cognizance of the several complaints regarding helicopter ticket bookings . . .

Taking exception to the agency's failure to file a report . . .

Taking serious note of news reports . . .

Talking about his journey, he said . . .

Terming the air quality in the national capital as poor and unsafe, she urged . . .

Terming the move rubbish, he pointed out . . .

Throwing a spanner in his aspiration . . .

Touching upon other problems, he said . . .

Turning to the issue of bribery . . .

Turning up the heat on his superior . . .

Underlining the importance of self-defence training for women, a judge ordered that . . .

Underscoring the need for brotherhood and togetherness, he said . . .

Using strong language, she said . . .

Voicing concern over the poor conditions . . .

Waking up to the growing problem of road rage . . .

Waking up to the need for making cabs safer . . .

Waking up to the need to conserve monument . . .

Walking away with other officials . . .

Waving signs and chanting slogans . . .

Winding up a debate on the Finance Bill, he said . . .

Wiping seat from his forehead, he said . . .

Wringing their hands in frustration and grumbling . . .

How to Start a Sentence -- Using 'PAST PARTICIPLES'

Aggrieved over the deaths, locals barged into the main buildings of the hospital alleging medical negligence.

Aimed at preparing a science-based plan for the conservation of aquatic species found in the rivers, Wild life institute constituted a team of experts to conduct study into behavioural pattern of aquatic animals.

Alarmed by the decreasing number of students at government schools, the education department has decided to conduct a pilot project in the district involving interactive teaching methods in classrooms.

Alerted, he quickly began distancing himself from the goon.

Angered over repeated accidents, many of them fatal, on the city flyovers, residents burnt the effigy of city administration.

Appointed this January, the panel has made shocking revelations.

Armed with stick, they ransacked ten houses.

Asked about the demand for his resignation, he shot back, "Anybody can say anything… I am satisfied with my work."

Asked about the future of the case he cited his success.

Based on his statement, the police have arrested the accused.

Blinded by rage, the individual loses reason and may end up harming himself or others.

Bombarded with questions on her winnability in the poll, a visibly irked candidate shot back, "Should I withdraw because I don't have enough numbers to with the election?"

Born into a family of modest means and high ideals, he hailed from a small town.

Broken by years of failure and mounting debt, she has scripted a remarkable turnaround.

Caught by both sudden pain and surprise, he first clutched his chest, unaware that he has been shot.

Celebrated annually, International Day of the Girl Child, highlights the challenges faced by young girls.

Charged with amassing wealth beyond known sources of income, he has for a month missed court hearing, prompting a judge to issue a non-bailable arrest warrant.

Confused at what had happened and scared, she first kept quiet.

Considered second in the line after president, he has resigned today by shocking all.

Depicted as king of devils, Ravana is said to have ten heads.

Diagnosed with a rare eye disease, she could not continue studies after class 12.

Dressed as soldiers, terrorists kidnapped nine foreigners.

Driven by the economic surge, ownership of cars has increased in the last few years.

Emboldened by thumping response from the people to his pubic gathering, he has decided to hold a mega rod show which will cover almost half of the city throughout the day.

Fanned by hot, dry winds, wildfires forced the evacuation of thousands of people.

Fed up of waiting for a road to link them to the main town, residents of the village took shovels and started digging a road for themselves.

Founded in 1909, the IISc had started with just two departments but today has over 40 departments.

Frustrated, he hurt himself.

Given a man of your standing, there will never be direct evidence for a criminal activity.

Given funds, he wants to develop a rocket.

Given that chocolate is an anti-oxidant and is supposed to be food for health, people don't say no to it as against a box of sweets dripping in clarified butter.

Given that we are living in highly contentious times, a festival that brings people together is certainly welcome.

Gone are the days when elections were won with muscle and money power.

Gone are the days when landlines were the only medium of communication between individuals.

Gone are the days when people had limited demands and lived a rather conservative lifestyle.

Gone are the days when simply throwing stones in a pond was a pleasurable activity.

Gone are the days when youngsters were glued to television.

Greeted with warmth and love, number of travelers frequenting Stockholm and its adjoining areas are increasing every season.

Heart-broken over not being able to make it into the Air force, a 22-year-old youth tried to kill himself.

Hit by a stray bullet while he was looking out of a window of his house, an elderly man was killed in the gunfight.

Known as a quiet worker he has endeared himself to the management.

Known for her fierce intellect, vigorous preparation and attention to detail, she has held various positions at central bank.

Known for its breathtaking views, Switzerland is known for its famous tourist spots.

Launched a few years ago, the scheme is known as RGDT.

Led by courageous mayor, the people set to achieve the objective with enthusiasm.

Located in the district of Nainital (India), Corbett National Park is a perfect place for nature enthusiasts and wildlife lovers.

Nabbed by police, he has seen the best and the worst of his life.

Nestled in the lap of picturesque mountains, our villages has emerged a role model for curbing rampant mining in its vicinity.

Paralyzed from the neck down for the past five years, he has nevertheless been administering his office every day, albeit with the help of technology.

Perched at an altitude of 1938 meters, Nainital is one of the most popular hill stations across India.

Perched atop a bus, he was greeted by a large number of supporters.

Questioned about whether beauty is skin deep or more, some people say that facial beauty matters, while others feel that character and qualities matter more.

Scared by the number of police officials who arrived at their house, the family is in a state of shock.

Shot at on her torso, she has injured her kidney.

Surrounded by mountains and with a very short runaway, the Toncontin airport is considered one of the world's most treacherous.

Terrified, he and she ran away.

Thrown out of the party, faced with charges of anti-party activities, he now faces with the biggest test of his political career.

Troubled by what he sees as growing division in the world, he tried to show that we are all one.

Wedged between China and India, Nepal depends heavily on India for the supply of essential goods.

Weighed down by huge debt and falling revenue, company recently announced suspension of its entire operations.

Wrapped in woolens, hands buried deep in pockets, they were looking something.

ADDITIONAL EXAMPLES:

Aimed at preventing road accidents . . .

Angered by the happening in city . . .

Asked as to how it could be a minor issue . . .

Asked if he knew the construction was illegal, he said . . .

Asked if the decision to video graph would not violate the secrecy of the meeting . . .

Asked to comment on the speculation of a leadership change in state, he said . . .

Asked to elaborate on the 'security implication' he said . . .

Asked whether a meeting would be convened shortly . . .

Built on river Thames . . .

Buoyed by his success . . .

Called "Reasons of defeat" the video features . . .

Concerned at dipping image of the judiciary system . . .

Concerned over his image coming under a cloud in the wake of corruption charge, he said . . .

Concerned over the Taj Mahal turning brownish and greenish in colour due to rising pollution levels . . .

Confused and with no one to turn to . . .

Disgruntled with the non-payment of dues . . .

Dressed in traditional costumes . . .

Dubbed as "Mr. Perfect" . . .

Elated with the number of people who came to participate in the program, the head of organizing committee said . . .

Enraged over what had happened . . .

Equipped with the production warrant . . .

Excited at the prospect of seeing Antarctica in his lifetime . . .

Faced with dissent in many cities . . .

Fed up with the shortage of cash . . .

Forced on the back-foot . . .

Frustrated with problems in her personal life . . .

Given the current challenging global and domestic growth environment . . .

Given the link between riots and serial blasts . . .

Given the magnitude of the devastation . . .

Given the recent threats, people will utilize . . .

Given the speed with which he delivered . . .

Hampered by adverse weather condition . . .

Known across the country for its . . .

Outraged by Team's near-certain exit from world cup . . .

Perturbed by the fact . . .

Queried about the consequences that his speech or actions may have, he said . . .

Regarded as the king of Everest . . .

Rendered jobless after the closure of shopping mall . . .

Saddened by shootings . . .

Strengthened by support . . .

Surrounded by a large chunk of barren land . . .

Unimpressed by explanation on breaking the guidelines . . .

Wanted by police in over 20 cases . . .

Worried at the large-scale devastation . . .

Worried with problems in the neighbourhood . . .

How to Start a Sentence -- Using '-LY Words'

Alarmingly, tens of thousands of households have no electricity connection.

Apparently, it was a suicide blast but police are still investigating to know the exact nature of blast.

Apparently, whatever we touch becomes a problem.

Basically, people have to be careful.

Basically, she is suffering from something that's called a jumper's knee.

Basically, tea encompasses processed and dried leaves of a plant species called 'Camellia sinensis'.

Certainly at this point, one cannot in anyway say your project has been a failure.

Economically, there doesn't seem to be a problem for his family.

Figuratively, optimists see the glass half-full, and pessimists half-empty.

Fortunately, both the political and bureaucratic leadership seemed determined to perform better than past years.

Fortunately, mankind has developed antibodies, which prevent the bacteria or virus from evolving at an early stage.

Fortunately, no damage was reported immediately.

Fortunately, the fire did not spread all along the area.

Fundamentally, new companies need to look at market opportunities.

Generally speaking, you are very obstinate.

Generally, exams foster an environment that places maximum stress upon students.

Generally, junk food looks attractive to people of every age.

Generally, lions do not actively participate in child rearing.

Generally, we are paid for our raw products by November-December.

Generally, yoga is thought of as performing of physical postures and breathing exercises.

Geologically, rocks are highly sheared and shattered in many areas.

Globally, 500 billion plastic bags are used annually.

Globally, many airlines are offering wi-fi for passengers.

Globally, more than 60% of clothes are made with synthetic fabrics.

Globally, mortality rates have decreased across all age groups over the past five decades, with the largest improvement occurring among children younger than five years.

Globally, suicide is much commoner among men than women.

Habitually checking for updates on social media can be disruptive and distracting.

Highly applauded, his victory has become one of the most memorable victories of recent years.

Historically, India witnessed seamless confluence of ideas, values, cultures and religions.

Historically, most countries have had to deal with humanitarian crisis.

Hopefully, if peace returns, I can go back to my hometown.

Hopefully, within a few minutes they will reach at the station.

Hopefully, you will be healthy again.

Ideally, a tiger needs around 15 square kilometer of area in natural habitat for daily activities.

Ideally, the functioning of the legislature should be marked by dignity and decorum.

Initially, 100 unemployed youths were given training in the field of computer programming through our center.

Initially, she was worried whether she would be able to shoot good photographs, post them and write stories.

Initially, we thought it was a bold step but gradually the ill-preparedness of the administration came through.

Internationally, every piece of jewelry is certified.

Lately, the government and people have started understanding the importance of diversity of nature.

Legally, it is impermissible to mix religion and politics in most countries.

Luckily, her husband is very patient and understands her schedule.

Luckily, we survived the attack.

Miraculously, the situation began to change.

Normally, youngsters feel strong and confident.

Notably, forest department has plans to open many forensic labs in the state.

Obviously, you can't just sit and say you won't do anything.

Occasionally, he has written about stories related to crime but he has never attempted a traditional detective story.

Ordinarily, a sound is created and heard when two hands are clapped.

Originally, all our projects were part of the government own developments programme.

Predominantly driven by the urban consumers, many items come under premium and super premium category.

Presently, there is no such proposal.

Proudly, he entered his new house.

Reportedly, the protestors attacked the police personnel, leaving a few cops injured.

Sadly and regrettably, most tyrants set a dangerous precedent by their insatiable desire to tarnish every Constitutional office.

Sadly, air pollution is on the rise.

Sadly, cartoons are no longer considered a powerful section of a newspaper.

Sadly, I was unable to explain my feelings to him.

Sadly, nobody seemed to be bothered about his whereabouts.

Sadly, the police appeared to side more with the attackers than those who were attacked.

Seemingly aware of polls due soon in a few states, chief minister proposed more money towards education.

Shockingly, none of the onlookers, not even the local police or civic volunteers posted on duty in the area took note of the ailing person's plight.

Shockingly, trekkers had not taken mandatory permission from district administration as well as forest department for high altitude treks.

Smartly, they finished their work just before the deadline.

Supposedly preparing for the medical entrance, he made some startling revelations.

Surely, we are reserved for something great!

Surely, we can walk the fine balance between privacy and openness on one hand and national security on the other.

Surprisingly, my journey till now has been almost effortless.

Swiftly, she left from the office.

Thankfully, he went in for the checkup without any delay and the doctor informed him that glaucoma was at an initial stage.

Traditionally considered the domain of politicians, inter-faith mass feeding is on the rise.

Traditionally, purchasing utensils of gold or silver for the household on festival of Dhanteras in Hindu Community is considered auspicious.

Traditionally, solar panels have been limited to the roofs of buildings, where there is space available and they are likely to get the most sun.

Tragically, ambulances with critically ill patients were stopped from reaching hospitals by agitators.

Typically, the expression of anger quickly degenerates into shouting, tantrums, and revenge.

Ultimately, we landed up paying from our own packets.

Undoubtedly, Harvard University is one of the best universities in the world.

Undoubtedly, life is not easy for people with diabetes.

Undoubtedly, we are going to win the final.

Unfortunately, due to an unhealthy lifestyle, there are times when heart diseases set in from an early age.

Unfortunately, people get captivated by money in many ways.

Usually, customers come to my shop in hurry and do not wait for bill.

Usually, river water disputes carry on for decades as grievance redressal mechanisms deal with recurring problems.

Usually, snowfall is followed by bright sunshine and clear weather.

Usually, the PWD informs traffic police before carrying out repair work on road so that vehicular movement could be managed.

Following is the list of '–Ly Words' that could be used to begin sentences:

absolutely, accordingly, actively, actually, additionally, admittedly, alternately, alternatively, anxiously, apparently, approvingly, approximately, arrogantly, assuredly, audaciously, automatically, barely, bashfully, basically, blissfully, boldly, bravely, briefly, brutally, calmly, carefully, carelessly, caringly, cautiously, certainly, cheerfully, chiefly, clearly, cleverly, commonly, comparatively, concurrently, confidently, consequently, conversely, correctly, correspondingly, courageously, crazily, cruelly, curiously, currently, customarily, dangerously, decidedly, definitely, deliberately, differently, diligently, doubtfully, easily, effectively, elegantly, eloquently, enormously, enviously, equally, especially, essentially, evenly, eventually, exclusively, fairly, faithfully, fatally, fearlessly, ferociously, fiercely, finally, firmly, fondly, foolishly, fortuitously, fortunately, frankly, frantically, freely, frequently, fruitfully, fundamentally, furiously, generally, gently, gladly, gleefully, gracefully, gratefully, gravely, greedily, habitually, happily, harshly, hastily, hazily, heatedly, hesitantly, honestly, hopefully, hopelessly, horribly, humbly, identically, immediately, importantly, impressively, initially, instantly, intensely, intently, irritably, justly, keenly, kindly, largely, lawfully, lazily, legally, lively, loudly, luckily, mainly, marginally, meaningfully, mercilessly, merrily, mightily, moderately, mortally, mutely, mysteriously, nearly, neatly, normally, occasionally, officially, openly, ordinarily, originally, painfully, partially, particularly, passionately, patiently, perfectly, persistently, playfully, pleasingly, politely, previously, primarily, principally, promptly, properly, punctually, purposely, quickly, quietly, rapidly, rarely, readily, regularly, relatively, repeatedly, resolutely, restlessly, righteously, rightly, roughly, rudely, sadly, safely, selfishly, sensibly, seriously, sharply, shyly, significantly, silently, similarly, skeptically, slightly, slowly, smoothly, softly, solemnly, specifically, speedily, sternly, strangely, strictly, stridently, strongly, stubbornly, subsequently, successfully, suddenly, superbly, surely, suspiciously, swiftly, terribly, thankfully, thoughtfully, tightly, timidly, tiredly, traditionally, truly, typically, ultimately, undoubtedly, unexpectedly, uniformly, unsteadily, unusually, valiantly, violently, weekly, wildly, willingly, wisely, worriedly

How to Start a Sentence -- Using 'PRONOUNS'

Everybody has his own ideas which he or she hates to change.
Everybody has something good in him.
Everybody is discontented with his or her lot in life.
Everybody knows the truth, let him or her tell it.
Everyone has the right to see dreams.
Everyone has to face one or other kind of pain in one's life.
Everyone left the place.
Everyone likes to have his or her way.
Everyone was falling on top of one another.
Everyone was lying on top of each other.
Everyone who is alive now will be dead sometime in the future.

It always feels good to pass on the joy.
It felt like a bad dream to watch our home being washed away in floods.
It has been more than a year since civic work for the bridge was started.
It is a Japanese robot.
It is a major concern that school buses that do not have any fitness certificates are used to ferry kids.
It is all yours doing.
It is better to fail with honour than win by cheating.
It is brand new car.
It is certain that he will come here.
It is clean.
It is completely unacceptable.
It is darkest day of his life.
It is depressing to wake up to a grey sky, smoky air and low visibility.
It is difficult to change what one learnt as a child.
It is easy to find fault.
It is fine.
It is for you to judge.
It is free of charge.
It is hers.

It is impossible to get this work done.

It is no thoroughfare.

It is not a prestige issue.

It is not my turn.

It is not the first time that he has left without informing anybody.

It is quite cold outside.

It is rare to see people who are extremely happy in both their personal and professional lives.

It is said that desires trigger more desires.

It is sullied.

It is ten o'clock.

It is the duty of every citizen of the country to follow rules.

It is the responsibility of the school management to keep students safe inside the school premises.

It is time to act.

It is time to depart now.

It is winter.

It is your teacher on the phone.

It rains. / It snows. / It thunders.

It takes a lot to serve the nation.

It was you who began the quarrel.

It weakened the economy.

These are merely excuses.

These are my books. / These books are mine.

These boys are very wise.

These girls are studious.

These jobs pay less than they did a decade ago.

They (people in general) say he has lost heavily.

They are committed to establishing rule of law.

They are easily identifiable.

They are not in a position to reveal anything about their jobs.

They didn't have very cordial relations for some years now.

They don't have money to feed their families.
They had a friendly talk.
They had already died when I arrived there.
They had argument over what to have for dinner.
They had no regard for ethics.
They had to pass through streets crowded with a mob of stone-pelters.
They have not received the salaries for the past two months.
They have sought my transaction details for the last past six years.
They held diametrically opposite positions.
They lit earthen lamps.
They made many rounds to the officials to remind them about the help promised by them.
They say that one of the local banks has stopped payment.
They seemed to be completely unaware of the ground realities.
They soon developed a liking for each other.
They were roaming in their without registration plate motorcycle, so that no one recognizes them.
They were surprised by her move.

This computer is ours.
This is a present from my student.
This is not the first time such directives have been issued.
This is not the proper way to go about things.
This is not the time for fault-finding.
This is the first time he has broken in to top 100 players.
This is your laptop. / **This** laptop is mine. **This** laptop is yours.
This work was not done the way it should have been.

Those are my books. / **Those** are your books. / **Those** books are theirs.
Those books are yours.
Those days of glory are today a faint blur in our minds.
Those images are fake.
Those who master time management skills can never be left behind.

How to Start a Sentence -- Miscellaneous

You can also begin a sentence with the following words/phrases:

ALTHOUGH
Although cycling is sometimes risky during the rains, it is an attractive challenge for adventure seekers.
Although he had been actively sailing for five years, his most recent voyage has made him realize how less he knows about the sea.
Although it is fast turning into a metro, this city lacks basic amenities.
Although light rainfall was recorded at some places, the weather mostly remained clear in the state.
Although not frequently reported, this is not an isolated event.
Although the rice mills are completely mechanized, the inward supply of paddy including its loading, unloading and feeding the plant with paddy stock is managed manually by the labourers.

AT
At 10, he was jovial and enthusiastic as other children.
At 86, he says he is counting his breaths.
At both places, the rescue operations are in progress.
At one point, he was totally broke.
At some point in our lives, we tend to turn to prayer, seeking divine blessings, to overcome problems.
At that point when I confronted the leopard, fear was the last thing on my mind.
At that point, he was so exhausted he couldn't run anymore.
At the end of the day, I am the captain.
At the most, I can lend you ten thousand dollars.
At the time of writing the exam, the biggest fear that a student has is, "Will I be able to complete my paper?"
At time, you may get cracked or itchy skin.
At times, I have seen women doing better than men in some of the physical endurance tests.

At times, I have to choose some handy food for my lunch because of my hectic work schedule.

At times, I was wondering if it was ever going to end.

At times, shopkeepers refuse to give a bill or even refuse to sell the goods if a consumer insists on a bill.

At a news conference, she said . . .

At every point, we could see . . .

At the crack of dawn . . .

BE

Be it known to all, that plot is subject matter of agreement.

Be it summers, spring or winters, they welcome tourists or their land all through the year.

Be it the end of a season or arrival, discounts offered by different brands and retailers are alluring for one and all.

BECAUSE OF

Because of the encroachments, pedestrians had no footpath to walk on and the drains were getting blocked.

Because of the greenhouse effect, global temperatures are rising, causing the Arctic and Antarctic ice caps to melt, which will make sea levels rise and flood low-lying countries.

Because of the heavy rains, many areas are repeatedly getting waterlogged.

BUT

But for your recommendation, I would not have got the job.

But not a one to put his feet down and relax, 78-year-old professor spent the day gardening.

But will anybody heed to this sage advice?

DESPITE

Despite ailments, she was very active till her last breath.

Despite all the measures the administration has taken, nothing has improved.

Despite ample snowfall, the water level in the lake has seen no surge.

Despite being an honest person, he has often been pulled down by critics for no reason.

Despite being sunny, a cold wave continued in most parts of the state.

Despite coming from a poor family, she was always cheerful.

Despite exhaustive investigations, not a single conclusive evidence of wrong doing was reported by any investigating agency.

Despite furnishing his identification proof, he was frisked like a common criminal.

Despite having seen financial hardships, he was never tempted by money.

Despite having spent millions of dollars on constructing operation theatres in community health centers, not a single surgery has been performed due to unavailability of surgeons.

Despite its repeated attempts to contact the CEO of the company over the phone, Amnesty International said it could not get any response.

Despite not having big faces in their advertisements campaign, their brand was accepted by the people.

Despite pain in my back, I must visit the office.

Despite playing with only 11 players and one goal down, we kept up the pressure on opposition's defence.

Despite repeated complaints, the authorities have failed to address the issue.

Despite repeated warnings, they went into the forest area and were attacked by a leopard.

Despite several limitations, they are trying their best to keep the animal shelter going.

Despite several warnings and health advisories, many people don't take precautions.

Despite so many teams working on the case, they have failed to make any headway.

Despite the ban, plastic is all over the place.

Despite the increasing penetration of internet and mobile phones in the communication field, postal service is still widely in use.

Despite the morning chill, voters came in huge numbers as the voting began at 8 am.

Despite the shutdown call given by trade associations, business was as usual in the city and markets remained opened.

Despite the squalid conditions in the overcrowded camps, many of the refuges say they are reluctant to return to their homes.

DUE TO

Due to busy lifestyles and unhealthy diet, obesity related problems have drastically increased.

Due to economic slowdown, our business has suffered a lot.

Due to his advanced age, he did not respond well to the treatment despite doctors' best efforts.

Due to inadequate infrastructure in government-run schools, parents in interior parts of the state send their children in public schools in towns.

Due to lack of sleep, you may feel drowsy, irritated or even depressed.

Due to negligence in track maintenance and inspection by ground staff, train derailments and other accidents occur.

Due to political pressure and other compulsions, these buildings cannot be demolished.

Due to poor condition of roads, people who travel in public transport including auto rickshaws and buses are having a hard time.

Due to the cold wave, the roadways department is seeing a decrease in number of passengers.

EVEN

Even as authorities are trying to finish repair works, there is a big question mark on the quality of hurried work.

Even as the mercury continues to dip each passing night, many homeless people have no other choice but to spend night out in the cold.

Even before a final schedule for the Winter Carnival chalked out, opposition for the carnival started.

Even if your qualifications are impressive, a glaring error on your resume could stand in the way between you and your dream job.

Even otherwise, our city is explosive.

EVERY

Every contestant is filing his/her nomination papers by exhibiting the numerical strength of their supporters.

Every life counts.

Every sunrise brings new joy, hope and something to look forward to.

Every time a blast rocks country, agencies are put on high alert.

Everyone in her family used to help her.

Everything I remembered was something I had wanted to forget.

Everything that we do, there is often a chance of failure.

EVER SINCE

Ever since a leopard killed a boy in the village, residents have been living in fear.

Ever since adulthood, his handwriting has been hurried and slapdash.

Ever since he was a boy, his father who was in the Navy used to make him wear his cap and from that age it became his dream to be a part of the Navy.

HAD

Had he got a good job, his mother would have distributed sweets to the neighbours.

Had I not given CPR in crucial seconds of his cardiac arrest, his chances of survival were close to nothing.

Had it not been for my friend, I **would have lived** in fear and harassment in foreign soil.

Had it not been for the facility of video calling, I don't know how we would have managed without seeing each other for long stretches of time.

Had the agitators allowed the ambulance to pass, her husband would have been alive.

Had the army not been alert, it could have resulted in communal riots.

Had the foreign minister **not intervened**, I **would have been forced** to go back to my native country.

Had there been an engine failure, the pilot would have sent distress signals to the control tower.

Had we reached even five minutes earlier, we probably would have been inside the stadium.

Had you approached senior officials and explained your plight, they would have received help sooner.

INSTEAD OF

Instead of competing with others, you should compete with yourself.

Instead of focusing on learning, students are more concerned about scoring good marks in exams.

Instead of grumbling about things that annoy you, just learn to avoid them.

Instead of just speaking about doing something, go out and do it.

Instead of saving lives speed breakers may increase risk of accidents.

JUST

Just a few days before traveling to USA, she had met her sister in Germany.

Just as nutritious food, regular exercise is necessary to keep the body strong.

Just over an hour of downpour left several streets of the city waterlogged.

LIKE

Like Erin, he claimed to know nothing of affair.

Like every year, he arrived in the city for festival.

Like everyone else, I was shocked by the controversy.

Like me, most people are not ready to go back.

Like my family, I was never against English as a language.

MANY

Many cases of theft have been reported in the past 10 months.

Many colleges suffer from deficiencies in infrastructure, clinical material and faculty.

Many complaints dared not go unaccompanied to police stations.

Many overcrowded jails have twice as many under-trials as convicts.

Many passengers throng railway stations everyday to board trains.

Many past incidents ran through my mind.

Many people are believed to have drowned when their boat capsized.

Many people are dependent on agriculture and animal husbandry for their livelihood.

Many people believe that their past successes mean they can succeed in the future.

Many people don't care about their health the way they do about their material belongings.

Many people have failed in school or other educational forums but have gone on to do well in life.

Many people have risen from deprived backgrounds to excel in their own fields.

Many places of the state have been receiving rain and hails since Monday afternoon.

Many poll booths saw people pouring in as soon as polling started at 8 am followed by a brief lull after which footfalls picked up again.

Many roads have become narrower because of encroachment on both sides.

Many roads pass through hills.

Many soldiers died anonymously in World War.

Many students did not have proper haircuts.

Many two-wheeler riders die for not wearing helmets.

Many urban families are forced into debt or sale of assets to meet hospitalization costs.

Many workers are employed in transportation and picking up river bed material from various rivers.

MAY

May all the evils in an around you vanish by the virtue of goddess!

May New Year bring joy, health, and wealth to your life!

May this festival be the harbinger of joy and prosperity!

May you life be prosperous and free form troubles throughout!

May your happiness by multiplied infinite times!

May your troubles burst away like the fireworks!

NEVER / NO / NOT / NO MATER / NO ONE / NOBODY / NOTHING

Never back off if you think you are on the right track.

No amount of compensation can be a substitute for life loss.

No charges against him were dropped by court.

No matter how many people we met, family is always the closest relationships we all have.

No matter, how much effort goes into planning, mistake may be made.

No new decision in the interests of wildlife has been taken in the past six months.

No one has assured us of our security and safety.

No one has done anything for our families.

No prior notice was given to us by the bank.

No special treatment should be meted out to any prisoner.

No tree, either big or small would be chopped off in our area.

Nobody knows when situations change.

Nobody likes being overcharged for things.

Nobody should be exploited.

Not just today, not tomorrow, this day will be remembered in our life for years to come.

Not long ago, we had organized a cleanliness campaign in the city.

Not much should be read into its absence at meeting today.

Not only does poetry help express our innermost and deepest emotions, it also tends to relax the minds.

Nothing can be done overnight.

Nothing could be cooked at his home for the last couple of days as he had no food-grains.

Nothing is more precious than independence and liberty.

Nothing repeats like the history.

ONCE

Once I had to stay for 50 hours without even drinking water in the peak of summer.

Once in the saddle, King moved with great speed to outmanoeuvre his rivals.

Once the final report is prepared, it will be sent to the higher authorities for further course of action.

Once the probe is over and he comes clean, he can be re-inducted.

Once they got possession of flat, they would sell it at a premium.

Once the child starts running fever . . .

Once you have had your fill . . .

OVER

Over the course of our lives, we acquire a collection of books.

Over the course of writing a book, she reached out hundreds of people.

Over the past three years, he has covered around 50,000 Km.

Over the years, human actions have posed a serious threat to wildlife.

Over the years, the world has progressed a lot in terms of materialism.

Over the years, they turned barren land into a lush green forest.

Over time, they will solve all problems.

RIGHT

Right at the start, my rear wheel was hit by another car.

Right from the very first day, we had been very clear in our stand and we remained unmoved.

Right now accident victims are in no condition to spell out in detail what happened.

SINCE

Since childhood, he has been a stubborn kind of person.

Since he had not paid the monthly rent for the past one year, the landlord locked his belonging inside the house.

Since the past two years, we have been facing water crisis, due to the declining levels of water bodies in our area.

SOME

Some bad elements made off with their luggage.

Some people have views on everything without understanding the situation.

Somehow, all of the tourists climbed up the nearest tree that they could find soon after seeing tigers.

THERE

There are a lot of people there who are against me.

There are around 9 million living species on earth.

There are certificates and plaques displayed in a glass showcase in my living room.

There are exceptional and compelling circumstances due to which we could not complete our project.

There are many cause of pollution.

There are many issues I am supposed to talk about with other attendees at the event.

There are moments in life we don't want to miss.

There are no clear winners in many wars.

There are no roads or proper health facilities.

There are some moments or situations in life that are unexpected.

There are some who are used to opposing everything we do.

There are special days round the year that are celebrated for all sorts of reasons.

There are times when the people feel overburdened because of poor time management.

There are variations in the statement of both the accused.

There are varied reasons and ways of celebrating New Year.

There are various kinds of refrigerators available depending on technology, size, capacity and price.

There had been an avalanche of rumours and conjectures.

There has never been a presidency that has done so much in such a short period.

There have been reports of angry customers clashing with shopkeepers.

There is a lot of moisture in the ground after recent rains.

There is a never-ending stream of cars on the road.

There is increasing focus on bringing down pollution around the monuments.

There is much we can and should together.

There is no electrification in our village and the roads are in terrible condition.

There is no lapse on the part of the law enforcement officers.

There is no more strength left in the victims even to cry.

There is no one here to address the issues faced by us.

There is no rule of law in the city and crime graph has steadily risen.

There is no substitute for hard work.

There is not much you can do about it.

There is nothing honorable about honor killing.

There is nothing more I could ask for.

There is nothing we haven't tried.

There is poor understanding among people about dangers posed by processed foods.

There is so much going on out there.

There is the need to take care of the suppressed, oppressed and depressed.

There should be clear-cut rules to reduce discretion by tax officers.

There should be no distortion of historical facts in the movie.

There should not be any discrimination.

There was a deafening noise and a jerk.

There was a mild fog in the morning which faded soon after as the day progressed.

There was fog coming through the window in the dining room.

There was gunfire and explosions everywhere.

There was no budget allocated for furniture of state-run primary schools.

There was no news about when his flight would depart.

There was not a shred of evidence against them.

There were nine pilgrims and a driver in the vehicle.

There were some heavy curses on his head.

There were tens of kids, but they weren't talking to each other, much less running around.

THOUGH

Though earlier incidents of atrocities on them took place, they were not at such extent that they are facing now.

Though never the one to give up easily, he made an exception this time.

Though no causalities were reported, some electronic and furniture were gutted in the fire.

Though the situation has improved over the last couple of years, much more needs to be done.

UNLIKE
Unlike a central banking system, which controls money supply, the creation of crypto-currencies is public.

Unlike his other batch-mates, he was mature, sincere, and followed instructions.

Unlike others, the restaurant sector usually has no support of subsidy, sops or loans.

Unlike religion, spirituality is expansive and borderless.

Unlike several other rivers of Kumaon, Kosi is not a glacier-fed river.

WHILE
While being examined by the prosecution in the case, he refuted all charges.

While confidentiality of cabinet matters needs to be maintained, this can't be an excuse for limiting access to all information for media persons.

While splashing water on herself, she slipped into the river.

While technology is bringing people closer, the sense of loneliness is growing.

While the audience got to their feet, ten people remained seated.

While the exact cause of derailment was still not known, the authorities ruled out the possibility of sabotage.

While they respect the jury's service, they are disappointed with the sentences, and intend to appeal.

While waiting at the airport, she kept posting messages on social sites.

ADDITIONAL EXAMPLES:
A decision to this effect was taken.

A few days ago he had returned his village with his wife and kids.

A week or so before any festival, preparations begin in full swing by people.

According to sources, residents are panicked by the rising water level in the rivers, especially after heavy rain on yesterday midnight.

Across the country, people are enjoying freedoms they haven't had in years.

Adhere to the highest standards of honesty, integrity, and accountability.

Afraid of getting caught, the men locked the house from outside.

Ahead of the peak summer season, authorities have identified hundreds of slums that are prone to water scarcity.

All the satellites had been put into orbit as planned.

All was silent in the examination hall as the examinees prepared to write their paper.

Almost every family harbours the dream of possessing a house they can call their own.

Amid this blame game, it's the area residents who continue to suffer.

Amid walkout by opposition, CM presented the Budget.

Among the prominent faces in fray in the last phase of the election are…

And to sit cross-legged under a tree!

Apart from stories from their past, they discuss current affairs.

Apprehensive of foul play, she went down and found him lying unconscious.

Aside from the occasional lottery ticket he doesn't gamble and doesn't not how to play poker.

Besides defending the borders of the country, the army had made several initiatives in the social services.

Besides saving the natural resources and diversity, conservation is helpful in generating revenues too.

Come Dec 30 and 2000 teachers will have to appear for an examination!

Come New Year and they earn $10000 each.

Delivery of swipe machines was getting delayed due to sudden increase in demand and shortage of these in banks.

Disappointment writ large on his face, he expressed dismay at the announcement of price hike.

Dispose the needles as per stipulated procedure.

Disputes, be it political or property related, are bad.

During sleep, we go through four to five cycles of deep sleep and dreaming episodes.

Each and every appointment should be made on the basis of merit and with transparency.

Each match from the first round itself will be very tough.

Elsewhere in the state, 100 people were rescued.

Entry of public and private vehicles is restricted on the several roads.

Ever before I finished school, I wanted to be a writer.

Far from flooded rural areas of country, people in capital are busy in enjoying festival.

Few things in the world are as powerful as hope.

First and foremost, I never advocated racial discrimination.

Foremost I want to thank you for your support.

Forget the neighbour, she hasn't talked her family members.

Gender-discrimination apart, an unjust law promotes crime.

Give back more than what you take from the nation.

Halfway through the lane, there was a fleeting but memorable scene.

Inside each one of us is a soul.

Irrespective of one's domain, an employee must have an expansive understanding of how latest technology will impact his/her area of work

Lack of timely actions by the authorities may lead to instill insecurity in the minds of residents.

Last season, they conceded almost two goals a game.

Leave alone some sleep; we are not able to get any peace either.

Less than a third of Earth's surface area is solid ground.

Let alone pay the installment; he is not even able to buy groceries for my family.

Let's put aside the 'corruption', there is no significant changes in others' problems.

Like many predecessors, new officer has promised to overhaul the system.

More than wanting to support me, they don't want to be with him.

Nearly half of humans believe in alien life and want to contact, a survey found.

Notwithstanding 10% rise in the number of students appearing for the board examination due next year, education department has decided to bring down the number of examination centers by almost 25%.

Now that he has quit, should others follow his example and step down.

Observation so far being is that the shoplifter has been arrested.

One of the main challenges globally is creating economic opportunities.

One year into the job, Mayor has been a reform.

Only after assurances from forest teams that the man-eating tiger would be trapped soon, the villagers relented.

Only after investigation is completed will further action be taken.

Other than making announcements, they have done nothing concrete in that direction.

Popular with tourists and teeming with night life, Connaught Place is a commercial hub.

Quite a few hotels do not have adequate parking space in this town.

Quite in contrast to the scene at our office was the opposition headquarters.

Second only to swimming, walking is said to be the best activity to keep you fit.

Set up recently on pattern of STF, ATS has started functioning.

Soon after the sugarcane harvest, there is little time left for the farmer to sow the wheat crop.

Straight from there, they went to office.

Strange as it may seem, police had provided perpetrator with a PSO.

Such a thing had happened.

Suggestions that have been submitted will be reviewed.

Thanks to technological advancement, various smart solutions are available for all stakeholders.

The moments I had spent with my friend flashed before my eyes.

Those who give bribe are as guilty as those who receive it.

Through his book, he has glorified my name.

Till about a decade ago, they use to live in caves in the mountains.

Till the time you are fully healthy, you should be kept in hospital for treatment.

Time and again, he has proved his mettle a fine performer.

Unable to face remarks of the fellow workers, he quit the job.

Under pressure to quit over his handling of internal security, home minister declined to do so.

Unhappy by the turn of events, he moved to the court.

Unless you have free press and if you don't have an independent judiciary, good government is not possible.

Unless your mind understands the knack of learning, you will never grow up in life.

Until a few years ago, he would migrate to big cities for a major part of the year for work.

Until he returns to home, we will remain worried.

Upon finding any issue in their physical appearance, many people go around inquiring for clinics.

Whether proposal is accepted by the SCT, remains to be seen.

Within a few minutes of reaching there, there was a blast.

World over, there are only 700 specialists in this field.

Some More Examples:

A few days back, in a similar incident . . .

A long time back . . .

About a kilometer into the road which leads to the office of the . . .

About their establishment in Italy, he said . . .

According to unconfirmed reports . . .

According to well-placed sources . . .

Ahead of the meeting . . .

All that remains to happen is the announcement of . . .

Amid battling militants in border . . .

Amid continuing violence in parts of city . . .

Among those turning up to watch match are . . .

And to top it all . . .

Angry over what they call a 'shoddy probe' . . .

Apart from facing discrimination . . .

Apart from focusing on major issues …

Apparently incensed over reports . . .

Apparently on the back-foot after an complaint was filed . . .

Around this time last year . . .

Ask about his views on the issue, she said . . .

At first . . .

At last count . . .

At the minimum/maximum . . .

At the same time . . .

At the start I told him . . .

Back from a visit to the U.S., he said . . .

Barely able to speak about what transpired on Wednesday morning . . .

Be it per capita income, literacy, health . . .

Because of the nature of court's directions . . .

But as happens so often . . .

But equally . . .

But what has left the landowner sleepless is the fact . . .

Clad in black coat, matching hat . . .

Completely at crossword, the officer said . . .

Consequent to the review of the events on . . .

Contrary to their earlier assertion . . .

Contrary to what government suggests . . .

Contrary to what one might assume, the phrase " . . ..." – . . .. – actually means . . .

Despite a number of initiatives taken by us . . .

Despite efforts by police to curb crimes . . .

Despite tribunal giving its final award . . .

Due to bad market sentiments . . .

Due to intensive efforts undertaken by us . . .

During the said timings . . .

During three rounds of deliberation . . .

Earlier in the day . . .

Earlier in the story . . .

Even as the Court appointed committee . . .

Every day at the crack of dawn . . .

Fresh in the memory of Germany, are the . . .

From the moment . . .

I am of the belief that . . .

Immediately following that . . .

Informed sources said . . .

Instead of addressing our problems . . .

It happened one day that . . .

Just around the time . . .

Latest in a series of storms . . .

Legend has it that . . .

Long and short of it is that . . .

Much to the complete amazement of those seated at the table, she announces . . .

Needless to say . . .

One line of inquiry is . . .

Over the years . . .

Picture this:

Prima facie . . .

Prior to this, on 10 September . . .

Prior to this, we provided . . .

Proud of the legacy that she left behind, he said that . . .

Put simply . . .

Rarely if ever . . .

Reluctant at first . . .

Sample this:

Simply because . . .

Six months into his terms as CEO . . .

So moved was the court by the plight of pedestrians . . .

So quick is the decline in numbers of vultures that . . .

Sources in the know revealed that . . .

Take, for instance the NSG . . .

The first thing that happened was . . .

The following important event was . . .

Their problem stems from the fact . . .

Thing took a turn when . . .

This apart/That apart/These apart . . .

This is not to suggest that . . .

This is with reference to your editorial, I agree . . .

Though it may appear on surface that . . .

Though the contents of the letter are not known, sources said . . .

Throughout the 30 or so minutes . . .

To ease tensions . . .

Top of the list, of course, are . . .

Towards the start of the journey . . .

Unable to anywhere near keep up with the pace . . .

Unable to come up with an apt word or an idea . . .

Unaware, what was happening inside . . .

Unbelievable as it may seem/sound . . .

Under attack on the issue of ID cards, governor said . . .

Under the plan . . .

Unlike a year ago, when . . .

Unlike expected . . .

Unlike in Australia . . .

Upon his return . . .

Whereas I am of the view . . .

Whether or not you should perform a task . . .

While addressing to gathered business community . . .

While chairing a high-level meeting . . .

While handing down the sentence, judge observed . . .

While on bail . . .

While pretending to count the cash . . .

Without giving much detail, he said . . .

Without wasting time . . .

Exercises: 1(A) and 1(B)

EXERCISE 1(A) –
Choose The Most Appropriate Answer:

acting on, against, apart from, before coming to power, considering the tension, despite repeated failures, if the authorities can't even repair, if we keep on increasing, in what has been described as, it is only through a public movement, now that, over the past couple of months, referring to his meeting, taking a strong view, under construction, whenever you look at, whether or not, with a view to, with five new cases reported, with our sense organs

01. .... and all sorts of adversities, they never gave up hope and continued to work hard with the 'never say die' spirit.

02. .... the population, how long can mother earth bear the additional burden?

03. .... something in hindsight, it always seems that it could have been done better.

04. .... prevailing at the village, top officials visited it and tried to allay the fears of the residents there.

05. .... specific technical and human intelligence about the presence of militants, security forces swooped down on their hideout.

06. .... the season's first major forest fires, around one hectare of biosphere and a few meadow have been gutted.

07. ...., political parties promise all sort of things to influence voters by means of their manifestoes.

08. .... of alleged irregularities in the use of funds allocated to the project, high court ordered a special audit to be done.

09. .... for the past two years, the building is expected to ready in another 3 months.

10. .... with police chief from across the country, the President said his administration was committed to national security.

11. .... earlier plans to increase prices by next month, we may do it earlier.

12. ...., the demand for a separate state has intensified.

13. .... he had started working, he should fund his expenses on his own.

14. .... the bruises on her head, she did not have any other fractures.

15. .... they do an autopsy, I don't know but I suspect they will.

16. .... conserve country's fauna, the government established the board of Wildlife.

17. .... in July, the number of dengue cases in the city has gone up to fourteen.

18. ...., we understand and experience the world.

19. .... that can we realize the dream of a cleaner state.

20. .... the roads that they dug up themselves, what will happen to the other roads?

ANSWERS TO THE EXERCISE – 1(A):

01. despite repeated failures | 02. if we keep on increasing | 03. whenever you look at | 04. considering the tension | 05. acting on | 06. in what has been described as | 07. before coming to power | 08. taking a strong view | 09. under construction | 10. referring to his meeting | 11. against | 12. over the past couple of months | 13. now that | 14. apart from | 15. whether or not | 16. with a view to | 17. with five new cases reported | 18. with our sense organs | 19. it is only through a public movement | 20. if the authorities can't even repair

EXERCISE 1(B) –
Choose The Most Appropriate Answer:

angry over, angry to the absence, as a result of, as per us laws, barring false promises, except for, for the second time in two days, if the party fails to give me a ticket, indicating that, it is diffIcult to live, it is distressing, it took him 15 years of hard work, just because, regardless, since there is, to celebrate festivals, to say that, with farmers threatening to block, with just some 15 days left, with the met office forecasting

01. ...., he was scolded for the negligence in his work.
02. .... for polling to be held, we have formed separated teams to reach out to the public.
03. .... with the same dignity and respect in the society once the police labels you a terror suspect.
04. .... constant efforts for conservation and habitat improvement, number of tigers is increasing in forest areas.
05. .... no electricity deep inside the forests, solar pumps are the best possible solution at present.
06. .... in the next two days, I have decided to contest as an independent.
07. ...., they have done nothing for the people of the country.
08. .... early polls seemed likely, the opposition party said it was ready for snap polls if the situation arises.
09. .... our area is fast turning into a haven for house robbers doesn't seem to be much of a misnomer.
10. ...., the presidency is term-limited to two four-year terms.
11. .... basic facilities like road and water in their area, people of as many as 60 villages decided not to cast their vote in the forthcoming assembly election.

12. .... he has been party president once, it does not mean that he would become president again.

13. .... rejection of his proposal, he refused to talk to him.

14. .... eliciting a few laughs, he has no other role to play in the function.

15. .... what we look like, where we come from, who we worship, we are human beings first.

16. .... squally weather with wind speed occasionally reaching 80-85 miles per hours in the next 24 hours in view of the cyclone, high alert had been sounded for officials in coastal area.

17. .... dairy and vegetable supplies it is not just governments but residents who will also feel the heat.

18. .... to see plastic bags choking up drains and littering up the roads.

19. ...., persistence and an enduring passion to write his book.

20. .... is everyone's right, but it should be kept in mind that no one else gets disturbed because of those celebrations.

ANSWERS TO THE EXERCISE – 1(B):

01. for the second time in two days | 02. with just some 15 days left | 03. it is difficult to live | 04. as a result of | 05. since there is | 06. if the party fails to give me a ticket | 07. barring false promises | 08. indicating that | 09. to say that | 10. as per us laws | 11. angry to the absence | 12. just because | 13. angry over | 14. except for | 15. regardless | 16. with the met office forecasting | 17. with farmers threatening to block | 18. it is distressing | 19. it took him 15 years of hard work | 20. to celebrate festivals

Exercises: 2(A) and 2(B)

EXERCISE 2(A) –
Rewrite the following sentences in correct word-order:

WRONG WORD-ORDER

01. By rural voters seemed government's satisfied the and with large, investment in infrastructure.

02. If with over a hundred prominent I had wanted, I could have formed to join politics a party politicians supporting me.

03. On a police team the accident, receiving information about rushed to the spot and sent the injured to hospital.

04. After take a written test physical qualifying the test they will also have to and some medical examinations.

05. With traffic surveillance, autorickshaw and tempo drivers little or no are seen constantly flouting rules.

06. Following a cordon and search operation, was intelligence inputs launched by anti-terror squat at the village.

07. If to a leader, I lend our support the follower of another leader will be hurt.

08. There in most city stretches and is increasing public transportation traffic congestion will only add to the woes of the people.

09. In three trains have been cancelled and, the route of 11 trains on the down line and 14 on the up line of the accident the wake has been diverted.

10. From being police, being falsely charged to tortured by he faced it all.

ANSWERS TO THE EXERCISE – 2(A) [CORRECT WORD-ORDER]

01. By and large, rural voters seemed satisfied with the government's investment in infrastructure.

02. If I had wanted to join politics, I could have formed a party with over a hundred prominent politicians supporting me.

03. On receiving information about the accident, a police team rushed to the spot and sent the injured to hospital.

04. After qualifying the physical test they will also have to take a written test and some medical examinations.

05. With little or no traffic surveillance, autorickshaw and tempo drivers are seen constantly flouting rules.

06. Following intelligence inputs, a cordon and search operation was launched by anti-terror squat at the village.

07. If I lend our support to a leader, the follower of another leader will be hurt.

08. There is traffic congestion in most city stretches and increasing public transportation will only add to the woes of the people.

09. In the wake of the accident, the route of 11 trains on the down line and 14 on the up line has been diverted and three trains have been cancelled.

10. From being falsely charged to being tortured by police, he faced it all.

EXERCISE 2(B) –
Rewrite the following sentences in correct word-order:

WRONG WORD-ORDER
01. Faced long queues, banks resorted to rationing of cash at many with currency shortage and branches countrywide.

02. At the thousands of daily wage labourers thronged, crack of dawn the crossing to find work in factories.

03. To, people in many areas this day walk several miles to fetch water for their daily needs.

04. There rain and snowfall in the state will be no in the next one week.

05. In the problems of the disabled, a move to focus on a committee was formed under leadership of cabinet minister.

06. In menace in the city, officials of the municipal corporation a bid to tackle the rising cases of dog and monkey have decided to undergo synchronized efforts to put an end to the hazard.

07. With vote bank is more, elections round the corner important for parties.

08. Irrespective at least he is discussing me of whether he is talking positive or negative,.

09. It for consumers to tell the difference between the real thing is not always easy and a fake.

10. To we need do much more yet, my answer is yes, to an extent, but to your question.

ANSWERS TO THE EXERCISE – 2(B) [CORRECT WORD-ORDER]

01. Faced with currency shortage and long queues, banks resorted to rationing of cash at many branches countrywide.

02. At the crack of dawn, thousands of daily wage labourers thronged the crossing to find work in factories.

03. To this day, people in many areas walk several miles to fetch water for their daily needs.

04. There will be no rain and snowfall in the next one week in the state.

05. In a move to focus on the problems of the disabled, a committee was formed under leadership of cabinet minister.

06. In a bid to tackle the rising cases of dog and monkey menace in the city, officials of the municipal corporation have decided to undergo synchronized efforts to put an end to the hazard.

07. With elections round the corner, vote bank is more important for parties.

08. Irrespective of whether he is talking positive or negative, at least he is discussing me.

09. It is not always easy for consumers to tell the difference between the real thing and a fake.

10. To your question, my answer is yes, to an extent, but we need to do much more yet.

****

About the Author

Manik Joshi, the author of this book was born on **Jan 26, 1979** at Ranikhet and is permanent resident of Haldwani, Kumaon zone of India. He is an Internet Marketer by profession. He is interested in domaining (business of buying and selling domain names), web designing (creating websites), and various online jobs (including 'self-publishing'). He is science graduate with ZBC (zoology, botany, and chemistry) subjects. He is also an MBA (with specialization in marketing). He has done three diploma courses in computer too. **ManikJoshi.com** is the personal website of the author.

Amazon Author Page of Manik Joshi:
https://www.amazon.com/author/manikjoshi

Email:
mail@manikjoshi.com

****

BIBLIOGRAPHY

'ENGLISH DAILY USE' TITLES BY MANIK JOSHI

01. How to Start a Sentence
02. English Interrogative Sentences
03. English Imperative Sentences
04. Negative Forms in English
05. Learn English Exclamations
06. English Causative Sentences
07. English Conditional Sentences
08. Creating Long Sentences in English
09. How to Use Numbers in Conversation
10. Making Comparisons in English
11. Examples of English Correlatives
12. Interchange of Active and Passive Voice
13. Repetition of Words
14. Remarks in English Language
15. Using Tenses in English
16. English Grammar- Am, Is, Are, Was, Were
17. English Grammar- Do, Does, Did
18. English Grammar- Have, Has, Had
19. English Grammar- Be and Have
20. English Modal Auxiliary Verbs
21. Direct and Indirect Speech
22. Get- Popular English Verb
23. Ending Sentences with Prepositions
24. Popular Sentences in English
25. Common English Sentences
26. Daily Use English Sentences
27. Speak English Sentences Everyday
28. Popular English Idioms and Phrases
29. Common English Phrases
30. Daily English- Important Notes

'ENGLISH WORD POWER' TITLES BY MANIK JOSHI

01. Dictionary of English Synonyms
02. Dictionary of English Antonyms
03. Homonyms, Homophones and Homographs
04. Dictionary of English Capitonyms
05. Dictionary of Prefixes and Suffixes
06. Dictionary of Combining Forms
07. Dictionary of Literary Words
08. Dictionary of Old-fashioned Words
09. Dictionary of Humorous Words
10. Compound Words in English
11. Dictionary of Informal Words
12. Dictionary of Category Words
13. Dictionary of One-word Substitution
14. Hypernyms and Hyponyms
15. Holonyms and Meronyms
16. Oronym Words in English
17. Dictionary of Root Words
18. Dictionary of English Idioms
19. Dictionary of Phrasal Verbs
20. Dictionary of Difficult Words

OTHER TITLES BY MANIK

01. English Word Exercises (Part 1)
02. English Word Exercises (Part 2)
03. English Word Exercises (Part 3)
04. English Sentence Exercises
05. Test Your English
06. Match the Two Parts of the Words
07. Letter-Order In Words
08. Simple, Compound, Complex, & Compound-Complex Sentences
09. Transitional Words and Phrases
10. Regular and Irregular Verbs

****